THE BEEHIVE STATE
100 DESTINATIONS YOU MUST VISIT

UTAH

TRAVEL GUIDE

DIANA L.
MITCHELL

© **Copyright 2024 - All rights reserved.**

The content contained within this book may not be reproduced, duplicated or transmitted without direct written permission from the author or the publisher.

Under no circumstances will any blame or legal responsibility be held against the publisher, or author, for any damages, reparation, or monetary loss due to the information contained within this book, either directly or indirectly.

Legal Notice:

This book is copyright protected. It is only for personal use. You cannot amend, distribute, sell, use, quote or paraphrase any part, or the content within this book, without the consent of the author or publisher.

Disclaimer Notice:

Please note the information contained within this document is for educational and entertainment purposes only. All effort has been executed to present accurate, up to date, reliable, complete information. No warranties of any kind are declared or implied. Readers acknowledge that the author is not engaged in the rendering of legal, financial, medical or professional advice. The content within this book has been derived from various sources. Please consult a licensed professional before attempting any techniques outlined in this book.

By reading this document, the reader agrees that under no circumstances is the author responsible for any losses, direct or indirect, that are incurred as a result of the use of the information contained within this document, including, but not limited to, errors, omissions, or inaccuracies.

Cover image: © LaserLens, Getty Images Pro sourced from canva.com

Table of Contents

Introduction 1

About Utah 3

   Landscape of Utah 3

      Dramatic Deserts and Towering Plateaus: The Southern Splendor . 3

      Urban Oases and Salt Flats: The Northern Contrast 3

      Majestic Mountains and Lush Valleys: The Northern Highlands 4

      The Colorado Plateau: A Geological Marvel 4

      The Diverse Basins and Ridges: The Western Range 4

      In Conclusion 4

   The Flora and Fauna of Utah 5

      Flora: A Desert Bloom 5

      Fauna: From Desert Sands to Snowy Peaks 6

      In Conclusion 6

   The Climate of Utah 7

      Seasonal Variations: A Year-Round Perspective 7

      Regional Climate Differences 7

      Impact of Climate Change 8

      Preparing for Travel 8

      In Conclusion 9

   The History of Utah 9

      Indigenous Heritage and Mormon Settlement 9

      Territorial Days and Statehood 9

      Economic Expansion and Modernization 10

      20th Century and Beyond 10

      Historical Landmarks and Legacy 10

      In Conclusion 11

Rocky Mountains 13

1. Logan Canyon 13
2. Ogden Valley 14
3. Ogden's Historic 25th Street 15
4. Lagoon Amusement Park 16
5. Red Butte Garden 17
6. Liberty Park 18
7. Mill Creek Canyon 19
8. Mount Olympus Trail 20
9. Wheeler Historic Farm 21
10. Snowbird Ski & Summer Resort 22
11. Big Cottonwood Canyon 23
12. Little Cottonwood Canyon 24
13. Bell Canyon Trail 25
14. The Living Planet Aquarium 26
15. Thanksgiving Point 27
16. Provo Canyon 28
17. Stewart Falls 29
18. Sundance Mountain Resort 30
19. American Fork Canyon 31
20. Timpanogos Cave National Monument 32
21. Cascade Springs 33
22. The Midway Ice Castles 34
23. Heber Valley Railroad 35
24. The Homestead Crater 36
25. Wasatch Mountain State Park 37
26. The Pfeifferhorn 38
27. Alta Ski Area 39
28. Brighton Ski Resort 40

29. Silver Lake 41
30. Solitude Mountain Resort 42
31. Donut Falls 43
32. The Utah Olympic Park 44
33. Park City 45
34. Deer Valley Resort 46
35. Jordanelle State Park 47
36. Mirror Lake 48
37. King's Peak 49
38. Bear Lake 50
39. Uinta Mountains 51
Basin and Ridge Region 53
1. The Spiral Jetty 53
2. Great Salt Lake 54
3. Antelope Island State Park 55
4. Stansbury Island 56
5. Bonneville Salt Flats 57
6. Silver Island Mountains Backcountry Byway 58
7. Utah Motorsports Campus 59
8. Tooele Valley Railroad Museum 60
9. Deseret Peak Wilderness 61
10. Pony Express Trail 62
11. Eagle Mountain 63
12. Utah Lake State Park 64
13. Springville Museum of Art 65
14. Nebo Loop National Scenic Byway 66
15. Little Sahara Recreation Area 67
16. Yuba State Park 68

17. Great Basin Museum 69
18. Territorial Statehouse State Park Museum 70
19. Fremont Indian State Park and Museum 71
20. Sevier Lake 72
21. Notch Peak 73
22. Crystal Ball Cave 74
23. Fish Springs National Wildlife Refuge 75
24. Topaz Mountain 76
25. Dugway Geode Beds 77

Colorado Plateau 79
1. Skyline Drive 79
2. Cleveland-Lloyd Dinosaur Quarry 80
3. Swasey's Beach 81
4. Arches National Park 82
5. The San Rafael Swell 83
6. Goblin Valley State Park 84
7. Bluejohn Canyon 85
8. Dead Horse Point State Park 86
9. The Maze 87
10. Canyonlands National Park 88
11. The Needles 89
12. Bear Ears National Monument 90
13. Edge of the Cedars State Park Museum 91
14. Natural Bridges National Monument 92
15. House on Fire Ruins 93
16. Hovenweep National Monument 94
17. Valley of the Gods 95
18. Mexican Hat 96

19.	Goosenecks State Park	97
20.	Moki Dugway	98
21.	Monument Valley	99
22.	Glen Canyon National Recreation Area	100
23.	Rainbow Bridge National Monument	101
24.	Lake Powell	102
25.	Buckskin Gulch	103
26.	The Wave Trail	104
27.	Coral Pink Sand Dunes State Park	105
28.	Sand Hollow State Park	106
29.	Zion National Park	107
30.	Cedar Breaks National Monument	108
31.	Bryce Canyon National Park	109
32.	Kodachrome Basin State Park	110
33.	Grand Staircase-Escalante National Monument	111
34.	Escalante Petrified Forest State Park	112
35.	Anasazi State Park Museum	113
36.	Capitol Reef National Park	114

Dear reader, thanks a lot for purchasing my book.

To help you plan your trip even more efficiently, I have included an interactive map powered by Google My Maps.

To access it, scan the QR code below.

Happy travelling!

A Note to Our Valued Readers

Thank you for choosing this travel guide as your companion for exploring the world.

I want to take a moment to address a concern you might have regarding the absence of photographs in this book.

As an independent author and publisher, I strive to deliver high-quality, informative content at an affordable price.

Including photographs in a printed book, however, presents significant challenges. Licensing high-quality images can be extremely costly, and unfortunately, I have no control over the print quality of images within the book.

Because these guides are printed and shipped by Amazon, I am unable to review the final print quality before they reach your hands.

So, rather than risk compromising your reading experience with subpar visuals, I've chosen to focus on providing detailed, insightful content that will help you make the most of your travels.

While this guide may not contain photos, it's packed with valuable information, insider tips, and recommendations to ensure you have an enriching and memorable journey.

Additionally, there's an interactive map powered by Google My Maps—an essential tool to help you plan your trip.

I encourage you to supplement your reading with online resources where you can find up-to-date images and visuals of the destinations covered in this guide.

I hope you find this book a helpful and inspiring resource as you embark on your next adventure.

Thank you for your understanding and support.

Safe travels,

Diana

Introduction

Welcome to *Utah Travel Guide*, your ultimate companion for exploring the diverse wonders of the Beehive State. From the rugged peaks of the Rocky Mountains to the surreal landscapes of the Colorado Plateau, this guide is your gateway to unforgettable experiences in Utah.

Our journey begins in the Rocky Mountains region, where adventure awaits amidst stunning natural beauty. Traverse the majestic Logan Canyon and be captivated by its towering cliffs and scenic vistas. Discover the tranquility of Ogden Valley, where outdoor enthusiasts can indulge in hiking, fishing, and more. Stroll along Ogden's Historic 25th Street and immerse yourself in its rich heritage and vibrant atmosphere.

For thrill-seekers, Lagoon Amusement Park offers adrenaline-pumping rides and family-friendly fun. Nature lovers can explore the botanical wonders of Red Butte Garden or unwind in the picturesque Liberty Park.

Heading further into the mountains, delve into the wilderness of Mill Creek Canyon or embark on the challenging Mount Olympus Trail for breathtaking views of the Wasatch Range. Experience pioneer life at Wheeler Historic Farm or hit the slopes at Snowbird Ski & Summer Resort, a paradise for skiers and snowboarders alike.

Venturing southward, encounter the wonders of the Colorado Plateau region, where ancient landscapes tell tales of time gone by. Marvel at the geological marvels of Arches National Park, with its iconic sandstone arches and dramatic vistas. Explore the labyrinthine canyons of Canyonlands National Park or stand in awe at the overlooks of Dead Horse Point State Park.

Discover hidden treasures like the mysterious House on Fire Ruins or the tranquil beauty of Natural Bridges National Monument. Hike through the otherworldly landscapes of Bryce Canyon National Park or immerse yourself in the splendor of Zion National Park, where towering cliffs and emerald pools await.

From the towering peaks of the Rocky Mountains to the sculpted red rocks of the Colorado Plateau, *Utah Travel Guide* invites you to embark on an epic journey through one of America's most captivating states. Each destination has been carefully selected to offer you an authentic and unforgettable experience, so pack your bags, lace up your hiking boots, and get ready to discover the magic of Utah like never before!

About Utah

Landscape of Utah

In *Utah Travel Guide*, we explore not just the destinations but the breathtaking canvas they are painted upon – the diverse and captivating landscape of Utah. This chapter delves into the varied terrains and natural wonders that make the Beehive State a showcase of the West's spectacular beauty.

Dramatic Deserts and Towering Plateaus: The Southern Splendor

Southern Utah is renowned for its dramatic desert landscapes and towering plateaus. From the intricate arches of Arches National Park to the vast expanses of the Grand Staircase-Escalante National Monument, the southern region offers an awe-inspiring meeting of earth and sky. The landscape is adorned with natural bridges, towering cliff faces, and deep canyons carved by the Colorado River, reflecting centuries of natural history. The area's unique culture is deeply influenced by its geography, where adventure sports, hiking, and the reverence for the land thrive.

Urban Oases and Salt Flats: The Northern Contrast

The urban centers of Salt Lake City and Ogden blend seamlessly with natural beauty. Salt Lake City, with the Wasatch Range as its backdrop, boasts an array of green spaces like Liberty Park and the Red Butte Garden, offering urban dwellers a slice of nature within the city. The Great Salt Lake and its surrounding salt flats, including the famous Bonneville Salt Flats, offer a starkly beautiful contrast to urban life, providing unique landscapes for exploration and contemplation.

Majestic Mountains and Lush Valleys: The Northern Highlands

Northern Utah is characterized by the majestic peaks of the Wasatch and Uinta Mountains and the lush valleys that cradle them. This region is a paradise for skiers, hikers, and outdoor enthusiasts, with world-renowned ski resorts and countless trails winding through alpine forests. The vibrant fall foliage transforms the landscape into a canvas of fiery colors, and the serene alpine lakes and streams offer tranquil retreats from the bustle of daily life.

The Colorado Plateau: A Geological Marvel

Eastern Utah is part of the expansive Colorado Plateau, a high desert region that includes some of the most iconic landscapes in the United States. This area is a treasure trove of geological marvels, from the deep canyons of Canyonlands National Park to the whimsical formations of Goblin Valley State Park. The region's rich archaeological history, visible in places like Bears Ears National Monument, adds a profound sense of timelessness to the rugged beauty.

The Diverse Basins and Ridges: The Western Range

Western Utah's basins and ranges offer a striking variety of landscapes, from the lush wetlands of the Bear River Migratory Bird Refuge to the desolate beauty of the West Desert. This area showcases the state's volcanic history, with ancient lava flows and craters dotting the landscape. The stark beauty of the Great Basin Desert, with its wide-open spaces and night skies free of light pollution, invites contemplation and adventure.

In Conclusion

The landscape of Utah is as diverse as it is breathtaking, from desert sands to mountain peaks, from urban parks to the vastness of the high desert. Each region offers its own unique beauty and challenges, inviting travelers to explore and become part of Utah's ongoing story. As you journey through these landscapes, remember that they are not just the backdrop but an integral part of the story of Utah.

The Flora and Fauna of Utah

In *Utah Travel Guide*, we journey not only through majestic landscapes and ancient formations but also delve into the vibrant tapestry of natural life that Utah nurtures. This chapter is dedicated to exploring the diverse flora and fauna that enrich the landscapes of the Beehive State, offering a glimpse into the resilient ecosystems that flourish here.

Flora: A Desert Bloom

Utah's flora is a study in adaptation and beauty, shaped by its rugged geography and climate extremes. From the arid deserts to the high mountain forests and the unique wetlands, each area presents its own botanical wonders.

Desert Vegetation: In the arid regions, hardy cacti, sagebrush, and juniper dominate. Spring brings a brief but spectacular display of wildflowers, transforming the desert floor into a canvas of color.

Mountain Flora: The higher elevations are home to coniferous forests, with species such as pine, aspen, and fir. These alpine areas burst into wildflower blooms in the summer, offering a stark contrast to the desert below.

Riparian Zones: Along the rivers and streams, lush riparian habitats support cottonwoods, willows, and a variety of grasses and shrubs. These green corridors are vital for wildlife and biodiversity.

Unique Species: Utah boasts several unique and endemic plant species, adapted to its varied environments. The state flower, the Sego lily, thrives in its desert landscape, while the blue spruce stands tall as the state tree.

Fauna: From Desert Sands to Snowy Peaks

The animal life in Utah is as varied as its landscapes, from the desert dwellers to the mountain inhabitants and the aquatic species in its rivers and lakes.

Desert and Plateau Wildlife: The arid regions are home to species such as the bighorn sheep, desert tortoise, and the elusive cougar. These animals have adapted to the harsh conditions, thriving in the ecosystem.

Mountain Fauna: The higher elevations shelter deer, elk, and the majestic moose, alongside predators like the black bear and bobcat. The varied birdlife includes eagles, hawks, and the state bird, the California gull.

Aquatic Species: Utah's rivers, lakes, and reservoirs are rich with trout and other fish species, supporting both wildlife and recreation. The Great Salt Lake itself is a crucial habitat for migratory birds, including the American avocet and the Wilson's phalarope.

Conservation Efforts: Utah is dedicated to preserving its natural heritage. Initiatives like the Utah Conservation Corps and protected areas such as the Bear River Migratory Bird Refuge and Zion National Park ensure the ongoing survival of diverse species and their habitats.

In Conclusion

The flora and fauna of Utah are integral to the state's mystique and splendor. They add a dynamic and vibrant layer to the already breathtaking landscapes, playing a crucial role in the ecological balance. As you traverse the destinations in this guide, take a moment to appreciate the natural beauty and rich biodiversity Utah has to offer. It's a reminder that our journey through Utah is not just about the places we visit but also about the living tapestry that forms the backdrop of our exploration.

The Climate of Utah

In *Utah Travel Guide*, the climate is a crucial element that shapes the experiences of each destination within the state. This chapter explores the climate of Utah, shedding light on how it influences the landscapes, flora, fauna, and the overall travel experience throughout the region.

Seasonal Variations: A Year-Round Perspective

Utah experiences a semi-arid to arid climate, though this varies significantly across its diverse landscapes, from desert to high mountain areas, bringing unique charms and challenges with each season.

Spring (March to May): This season sees a gradual warming across the state. Early spring in Utah's high country may still be snowy and cold, while the deserts begin to warm up. This is a time of blooming wildflowers in the desert and melting snow in the mountains, creating vibrant and contrasting landscapes.

Summer (June to August): Summers in Utah can be hot, especially in the desert regions where temperatures often soar above 100°F (38°C). The mountain areas offer a cooler escape, with pleasant temperatures ideal for hiking and outdoor exploration.

Fall (September to November): Autumn brings a cooling trend, with the desert's intense heat giving way to comfortable days and crisp nights. In the mountains, the foliage turns to vivid hues of orange, red, and yellow, offering spectacular scenic drives and hiking experiences.

Winter (December to February): Winters vary greatly across Utah. The desert areas remain relatively mild, while the mountain regions receive significant snowfall, transforming into prime destinations for skiing and snowboarding enthusiasts.

Regional Climate Differences

The climate in Utah exhibits notable differences depending on the region:

Desert Areas: Including much of southern Utah, these areas experience mild winters and extremely hot summers. Precipitation is low, resulting in arid landscapes.

Mountain Regions: The higher elevations, such as the Wasatch Range, see cooler summers and cold, snowy winters. These areas are a haven for winter sports and provide a respite from the summer heat.

Great Salt Lake Effect: The area around the Great Salt Lake experiences a unique microclimate, with the lake influencing weather patterns to create more precipitation in nearby regions.

Impact of Climate Change

Climate change is having an impact on Utah, with increased temperatures affecting snowpack levels in the mountains and potentially altering the desert ecosystems. These changes are being closely monitored to gauge their long-term effects on Utah's natural environment and tourism industry.

Preparing for Travel

When planning a visit to Utah, considering the seasonal variations is crucial:

Spring and Summer: Prepare for warm to hot temperatures, especially in desert areas. Light clothing, sunscreen, and plenty of water are essentials.

Fall: Pack layered clothing to accommodate warm days and cooler nights, especially if you're exploring both desert and mountain regions.

Winter: Warm clothing and gear for snow activities are essential for those heading to the mountains, while lighter layers may suffice for desert regions.

In Conclusion

The climate of Utah enriches the state's allure, offering a dynamic setting that shifts with the seasons. Whether exploring the desert landscapes under the summer sun, witnessing the autumnal change in the mountains, or enjoying winter sports in the high country, understanding Utah's climate will enhance your experience and help you prepare for an unforgettable journey.

The History of Utah

In *Utah Travel Guide*, the history of Utah is not merely a backdrop but a fundamental part of the state's identity. This chapter guides you through time, unveiling the rich historical tapestry that has shaped Utah into the unique state it is today.

Indigenous Heritage and Mormon Settlement

Long before European exploration, Utah was the home of diverse Indigenous peoples, including the Ute, Navajo, and Paiute tribes, among others. Their cultures and traditions deeply influenced the region, leaving a lasting legacy on the land.

The mid-19th century heralded a new chapter with the arrival of Mormon pioneers, led by Brigham Young. Seeking a sanctuary from religious persecution, they founded Salt Lake City in 1847. This marked the beginning of the large-scale settlement by members of The Church of Jesus Christ of Latter-day Saints (LDS Church), significantly shaping the region's demographic and cultural landscape.

Territorial Days and Statehood

Utah's path to statehood was complex and intertwined with issues such as polygamy, which the LDS Church initially practiced. After a series of negotiations with the federal government and the official discontinuation of polygamy, Utah was admitted as the 45th state of the Union in 1896.

Economic Expansion and Modernization

Throughout the late 19th and early 20th centuries, Utah experienced significant economic growth and diversification. Mining, particularly of salt, copper, and coal, played a crucial role in the state's economy. This period also saw the expansion of the railroad, further integrating Utah into the national market and fostering urban development.

20th Century and Beyond

The 20th century brought technological and educational advancement to Utah, with the establishment of research institutions and a growing tech industry in what is now known as the Silicon Slopes. Utah's scenic beauty and outdoor recreational opportunities also began to attract tourism, further diversifying the state's economy.

Utah continued to be a site of social and cultural evolution, with the LDS Church playing a significant role in the state's politics and community life. The state has also made strides in environmental conservation, preserving its unique landscapes through the creation of national parks and monuments.

Historical Landmarks and Legacy

Utah is rich with historical landmarks that tell the story of its diverse past. From the ancient rock art in Nine Mile Canyon to the historic Temple Square in Salt Lake City, and the picturesque Monument Valley on the Navajo Nation reservation, Utah offers a deep connection to both its Indigenous and pioneer heritage.

In Conclusion

Understanding the history of Utah is essential to appreciating its present. From its Indigenous roots through its pioneer settlement, to its role in the broader tapestry of American history, Utah's story is one of perseverance, innovation, and cultural convergence. As you explore the destinations in this guide, take a moment to consider the historical significance of each location and how it has contributed to the rich tapestry that is Utah today.

Rocky Mountains

1. **Logan Canyon**

Stretching approximately 41 miles from the city of Logan to Garden City at Bear Lake, this canyon offers a diverse landscape that captivates visitors with its rugged cliffs, dense forests, and riverine ecosystems.

The drive through Logan Canyon itself is a visual feast. U.S. Highway 89, which winds through the canyon, has been designated as a National Scenic Byway, acknowledging the exceptional beauty of its natural landscapes. Each turn in the road reveals stunning vistas, from towering limestone cliffs and dense stands of pine and aspen trees to the serene waters of the Logan River flowing alongside. The changing seasons add to the canyon's allure, with vibrant wildflowers in spring and summer, a kaleidoscope of fall foliage, and a serene blanket of snow in winter.

Logan Canyon is a haven for outdoor enthusiasts. Hiking trails of all levels wind through the canyon, leading to such natural wonders as the Wind Caves, a set of natural limestone arches and caves formed by the erosive forces of wind and water. Another highlight is the Crimson Trail, which offers panoramic views of the canyon's geological formations and the Logan River. For those looking for a less strenuous activity, the Riverside Nature Trail provides a gentle walk with interpretive signs describing the local flora and fauna.

The Logan River, a centerpiece of the canyon, is renowned for its excellent trout fishing, drawing anglers from across the region. The river's clear, cold waters are home to a variety of fish species, including cutthroat trout, rainbow trout, and brown trout, offering both challenge and reward for fishing enthusiasts.

In addition to its natural attractions, Logan Canyon is steeped in history. The canyon was a significant travel route for Native American tribes, including the Shoshone, who traversed its paths long before European settlers arrived. In the late 19th and early 20th centuries, the canyon played a role in the development of the logging industry in northern Utah, remnants of which can still be seen in the form of old logging roads and railroad grades.

2. Ogden Valley

Ogden Valley, nestled in the heart of the Wasatch Range in northern Utah, is a gem of natural beauty and outdoor recreation. One of the most striking features of Ogden Valley is its versatility as a destination for outdoor activities, regardless of the season. In the winter, the valley transforms into a winter sports paradise, with three major ski resorts: Snowbasin, Powder Mountain, and Nordic Valley. Snowbasin, renowned for its expansive terrain and luxurious lodges, was one of the venues for the 2002 Winter Olympics, offering some of the best downhill skiing in Utah. Powder Mountain prides itself on its vast acreage and uncrowded slopes, providing a more laid-back skiing experience. Nordic Valley, though smaller, offers a family-friendly atmosphere with night skiing options, making it accessible for beginners and families.

Come summer, the landscape shifts dramatically, revealing lush greenery, wildflowers, and the sparkling waters of Pineview Reservoir. The reservoir becomes a hub of activity, attracting visitors for boating, fishing, swimming, and paddleboarding. The clear, cool waters are ideal for escaping the summer heat, while the surrounding beaches provide perfect spots for picnics and relaxation.

Beyond water sports, Ogden Valley is crisscrossed with trails for hiking, mountain biking, and horseback riding, offering breathtaking views and access to remote natural areas. Trails like the Skyline Trail offer challenging hikes with rewarding vistas of the valley and beyond. For those interested in mountain biking, the valley boasts some of the best trails in the state, with routes varying in difficulty to accommodate all skill levels.

Ogden Valley also holds a rich cultural and historical significance. The town of Huntsville is home to the oldest continuously operating bar in Utah, the Shooting Star Saloon, offering a glimpse into the valley's pioneering spirit. The valley's history is further celebrated in local festivals and events, including the annual Balloon Festival, which fills the sky with colorful hot air balloons, creating a mesmerizing spectacle against the backdrop of the Wasatch Range.

3. Ogden's Historic 25th Street

Ogden's Historic 25th Street, often referred to as "Two-Bit Street," is a vibrant microcosm of Utah's broader historical and cultural tapestry. Stretching three blocks from Union Station to Washington Boulevard, this historic district is a testament to Ogden's storied past, evolving from its early days as a lawless frontier town to its current status as a lively hub of culture, cuisine, and entertainment. Once the heart of a bustling railroad community, 25th Street has witnessed the ebb and flow of Ogden's fortunes, playing host to infamous figures, travelers, and immigrants who left an indelible mark on the city's identity.

Today, Historic 25th Street thrives as a dynamic destination, where the echoes of the past blend seamlessly with the energy of the present. The street is lined with beautifully restored buildings that house an eclectic mix of independent shops, art galleries, restaurants, and bars, each adding its unique flavor to the street's vibrant atmosphere. The architectural diversity along the street, from Victorian to early 20th-century styles, reflects the various eras of Ogden's development, inviting visitors to take a step back in time as they explore the area.

Dining on 25th Street offers an array of options, from casual eateries to upscale restaurants, serving everything from traditional American fare to international cuisine. The street's nightlife is equally diverse, with bars and clubs providing live music, entertainment, and a glimpse into the local social scene.

Cultural events and festivals regularly animate the street, drawing both locals and tourists to celebrate Ogden's rich heritage and community spirit. From farmers' markets to art strolls and holiday celebrations, these events offer opportunities to engage with the local culture and artisans.

Ogden's Historic 25th Street is more than just a street; it's a living museum, a center of community life, and a destination for those seeking to experience the authentic soul of the city. Its successful transformation from a notorious railroad thoroughfare to a bustling cultural district symbolizes Ogden's resilience and adaptive spirit. For anyone visiting Ogden, a stroll down Historic 25th Street is an essential experience, offering a taste of the city's past, present, and future.

4. Lagoon Amusement Park

Lagoon Amusement Park, nestled in Farmington, Utah, just north of Salt Lake City, is a beacon of fun and excitement for families and thrill-seekers alike. Established in 1886, Lagoon has grown from a lakeside resort of yesteryear into one of the Rocky Mountain's most beloved amusement parks, combining classic charm with modern thrills across its sprawling 95-acre site. It's a place where generations of visitors have created lasting memories, underscored by the park's motto, "It's What Fun Is!"

Lagoon boasts over 50 rides, ranging from heart-pounding roller coasters to gentle options for the littlest adventurers, ensuring that every visitor finds their slice of fun. Among its most iconic rides is the Cannibal, which drops riders from a 208-foot tower into an underground tunnel at speeds up to 70 miles per hour, offering an adrenaline rush unlike any other. The Wicked, with its vertical lift and high-speed twists, and the classic wooden coaster, Roller Coaster, one of the oldest operating wooden coasters in the world, add to the park's rich assortment of thrill rides.

Beyond the roller coasters, Lagoon offers a diverse array of attractions suitable for all ages. Pioneer Village, located within the park, is a living museum where guests can step back in time to experience life in the Old West. The park's waterpark, Lagoon A Beach, provides a refreshing escape with its six acres of swimming pools, slides, and a lazy river, perfect for cooling off on hot summer days.

Lagoon is also home to a variety of entertainment options, including live performances, musicals, and magic shows, adding a cultural dimension to the amusement park experience. Seasonal events, like Frightmares in October, bring a festive atmosphere to the park, with haunted houses, spooky decorations, and themed entertainment that attract visitors looking for both thrills and chills.

With a commitment to creating a family-friendly environment that offers something for everyone, Lagoon continues to expand and evolve, introducing new rides and attractions while preserving the historical elements that have made it a cherished destination for over a century.

5. Red Butte Garden

Red Butte Garden, located on the eastern edge of Salt Lake City, Utah, against the beautiful backdrop of the Wasatch Mountain Range, is a renowned botanical garden and arboretum that offers a serene and educational escape from the bustling city life. Sprawling over 100 acres, with more than five miles of hiking trails, this meticulously maintained garden is part of the University of Utah and serves as a living museum dedicated to the study and appreciation of the world's plant life.

Established in 1985, Red Butte Garden is recognized for its extensive collections of botanical and horticultural plants, with a focus on showcasing species native to the Intermountain West. The garden's diverse ecosystems range from lush herb and vegetable gardens to arid deserts, displaying a vast array of plant diversity that educates and inspires visitors about the importance of conservation and sustainable gardening practices.

One of the garden's highlights is the thematic arrangement of its gardens, including the Water Conservation Garden, which demonstrates the beauty and feasibility of low-water landscaping, and the Children's Garden, designed to spark curiosity and love for nature in younger visitors. The Rose Garden is a fragrant and colorful spectacle, featuring a stunning variety of roses that bloom beautifully against Utah's mountainous landscape.

Red Butte Garden is also famous for its outdoor concert series, hosting an array of performances ranging from classical music to contemporary bands in its amphitheater. This unique venue allows guests to enjoy live music amidst the natural beauty of the garden, creating unforgettable summer evenings under the stars.

Seasonal events, such as the springtime Blooms Festival and the holiday-themed Garden After Dark, offer visitors unique experiences that highlight the changing beauty of the garden throughout the year. Educational programs, workshops, and lectures are also available, providing valuable information on horticulture, conservation, and art.

6. Liberty Park

Liberty Park, Salt Lake City's second-largest public park, is a sprawling 80-acre oasis of greenery and recreation in the heart of Utah's capital. This historic park, established in 1881, has long served as a communal gathering place, offering a peaceful retreat for residents and visitors alike amidst the urban landscape. Its well-preserved environment and array of amenities make it a beloved destination for leisure and outdoor activities year-round.

At the core of Liberty Park's appeal is its blend of natural beauty and recreational facilities. The park features a large pond where ducks and geese glide gracefully across the water, adding to the serene atmosphere. Paths wind through the park, inviting joggers, cyclists, and walkers to enjoy the tranquil surroundings and lush, meticulously maintained landscapes. Large, old-growth trees provide ample shade, creating a perfect setting for picnics, reading, or simply relaxing under the canopy.

Liberty Park is not just a haven for tranquility and passive recreation; it's also equipped with a variety of facilities to engage visitors of all ages. The park houses tennis courts, volleyball courts, and a swimming pool, catering to sports enthusiasts. For families, the park offers playgrounds and the Seven Canyons Fountain, a water feature representing Utah's major canyons, where children can splash and play.

One of the park's highlights is the Tracy Aviary, located within its grounds. As one of the oldest aviaries in the United States, Tracy Aviary provides an up-close look at various bird species, both native and exotic. It serves as an educational resource, offering insights into avian conservation and habitat preservation.

Liberty Park also plays host to a variety of community events throughout the year, including outdoor concerts, cultural festivals, and craft markets. These events reflect the diverse fabric of Salt Lake City's community and offer visitors a taste of local traditions and creativity.

In essence, Liberty Park is more than just a park; it's a vibrant community center where nature, recreation, and culture intersect. Whether seeking a space for active play, a quiet corner for reflection, or a venue to experience local events, Liberty Park offers a welcoming space for all.

7. Mill Creek Canyon

Mill Creek Canyon, located just a few miles east of Salt Lake City, Utah, is a verdant natural retreat that beckons outdoor enthusiasts with its scenic beauty and myriad recreational opportunities. This canyon, part of the Wasatch National Forest, offers an easily accessible escape into nature, where visitors can immerse themselves in the tranquil beauty of the Rocky Mountains. The canyon is renowned for its lush forests, vibrant wildflowers, cascading streams, and a network of trails that cater to hikers, mountain bikers, and nature lovers of all skill levels.

One of the most appealing aspects of Mill Creek Canyon is its year-round accessibility, providing a picturesque backdrop for a variety of outdoor activities. During the warmer months, the canyon's extensive trail system becomes a haven for hikers and mountain bikers. Trails range from easy strolls along the canyon floor to more challenging hikes that ascend to breathtaking overlooks and serene mountain lakes. The Pipeline Trail is particularly popular, offering panoramic views of the Salt Lake Valley with minimal elevation gain, making it suitable for families and casual hikers.

In the winter, Mill Creek Canyon transforms into a winter wonderland, attracting cross-country skiers and snowshoers. The quiet beauty of the snow-covered landscape offers a serene setting for exploring the canyon's natural wonders under a blanket of snow. The road through the canyon remains open year-round, providing access to trailheads and picnic areas, even in the winter months.

Another unique feature of Mill Creek Canyon is the opportunity for off-leash dog walking on odd-numbered days, making it a favorite destination for pet owners. Dogs can freely explore the trails and streams, ensuring a joyful experience for both pets and their owners.

Mill Creek Canyon is not only a recreational treasure but also an ecological haven. It serves as a critical watershed for Salt Lake City, and its pristine environment is home to a diverse array of wildlife, including deer, moose, and various bird species. This delicate ecosystem underscores the importance of conservation efforts and responsible recreation to preserve the canyon's natural beauty for future generations.

8. Mount Olympus Trail

The Mount Olympus Trail is one of the most iconic hiking routes in the Salt Lake Valley, offering an exhilarating climb to the summit of Mount Olympus, a prominent peak that towers over the eastern landscape of Salt Lake City, Utah. This challenging trail, beloved by locals and visitors alike, is renowned for its steep ascent, rewarding adventurers with unparalleled panoramic views of the Salt Lake Valley, the Great Salt Lake, and the surrounding Wasatch Range.

Spanning approximately 3.75 miles one way, the trail gains nearly 4,000 feet in elevation, making it a strenuous hike that demands physical fitness and determination. Despite its difficulty, the trail attracts a steady stream of hikers year-round, drawn by the promise of natural beauty and the sense of accomplishment that comes with reaching the summit.

The journey begins in a lush, lower-elevation environment, winding through scrub oak and mountain mahogany. As hikers ascend, the vegetation transitions to fir and aspen forests, offering occasional shade and a reprieve from the sun's intensity. The trail's higher segments navigate rocky terrain and steep switchbacks, challenging even seasoned hikers.

One of the trail's highlights is the final push to the summit, where hikers navigate a steep, rocky ridge. This section requires careful footing and a head for heights, but the effort is amply rewarded upon reaching the top. The summit of Mount Olympus offers breathtaking 360-degree views that encapsulate the rugged beauty of Utah's landscape, providing a memorable backdrop for photos and a moment of reflection.

The Mount Olympus Trail is not only a test of physical endurance but also an immersive experience in the natural world, offering intimate encounters with the flora and fauna of the Wasatch Mountains. It's a reminder of the wild, untamed beauty that lies just beyond the city's boundaries, inviting hikers to explore the heights and depths of Utah's majestic outdoors. Whether seeking a challenging workout or the serenity of nature, the Mount Olympus Trail delivers an unforgettable adventure.

9. Wheeler Historic Farm

Wheeler Historic Farm, nestled in the heart of Murray, Utah, is a step back in time to the state's agricultural past. This fully operational turn-of-the-century farm offers visitors a unique glimpse into the day-to-day operations of a late 19th-century Utah farmstead. Spread over 75 acres of natural landscape, Wheeler Farm is more than a museum; it's a vibrant, interactive experience that connects people with the agricultural heritage and rural life of the region.

The farm stands as a testament to Utah's farming history, meticulously preserved to maintain the authenticity of the period. Visitors can explore the original Wheeler family farmhouse, which has been restored to its historical condition, offering insights into the living conditions and lifestyles of early Utah settlers. The property also features a collection of vintage farm equipment and buildings, including barns, a dairy, and a blacksmith shop, each contributing to the narrative of early agricultural practices.

One of the highlights of Wheeler Historic Farm is the opportunity for hands-on experiences. Guests can participate in daily farm activities such as cow milking, animal feeding, and hay wagon rides, providing a tangible connection to the farming processes. The farm's animals, including cows, horses, chickens, and sheep, play a pivotal role in these activities, delighting visitors of all ages.

Beyond its educational offerings, Wheeler Historic Farm serves as a community hub, hosting events throughout the year like farmers markets, holiday celebrations, and historical demonstrations. These events not only celebrate the farm's rich history but also bring together the community in a setting that is both scenic and serene.

Wheeler Historic Farm is an invaluable resource for understanding Utah's agricultural evolution and its impact on the community. It provides a peaceful escape from the modern world, allowing visitors to immerse themselves in the simplicity and beauty of farm life. For families, history enthusiasts, and those seeking a connection with nature, Wheeler Historic Farm offers an enriching and educational experience that celebrates Utah's agrarian roots and enduring spirit.

10. Snowbird Ski & Summer Resort

Snowbird Ski & Summer Resort, nestled in the heart of Utah's majestic Wasatch Mountains, is a premier destination for outdoor enthusiasts year-round. Located in Little Cottonwood Canyon, just a short drive from Salt Lake City, Snowbird offers a stunning natural backdrop, world-class skiing, and a plethora of summer activities, making it a favorite among both locals and visitors from around the globe.

During the winter months, Snowbird transforms into a skier's paradise. With an average annual snowfall of over 500 inches of the finest, lightest powder, the resort boasts a wide range of terrain catering to all skill levels. From gentle, groomed runs for beginners to challenging bowls and chutes for the more adventurous, Snowbird ensures an exhilarating experience for every skier and snowboarder. The resort's Aerial Tram, which ascends to the summit of Hidden Peak, offers not only a unique ride but also provides access to some of the most breathtaking vistas and ski runs in the region.

As the snow melts and summer takes hold, Snowbird seamlessly transitions into a vibrant summer resort. The mountain's rugged terrain becomes a haven for hikers and mountain bikers, with trails that wind through wildflower-strewn meadows and past cascading streams. The resort also offers a range of family-friendly activities, including an alpine slide, mountain coaster, and a scenic tram ride that offers panoramic views of the surrounding mountain ranges and valleys.

Snowbird Ski & Summer Resort is not just about outdoor adventure; it also offers top-notch amenities, including luxurious accommodations, fine dining, and a world-class spa. Whether visitors are looking to relax after a day on the slopes or enjoy a gourmet meal with a view, Snowbird provides a comprehensive resort experience that combines the beauty of the Wasatch Mountains with unparalleled hospitality and service.

For those seeking the thrill of winter sports or the serenity of mountain summers, Snowbird Ski & Summer Resort embodies the best of both worlds. It stands as a testament to Utah's natural beauty and its reputation as a premier destination for outdoor recreation.

11. Big Cottonwood Canyon

Big Cottonwood Canyon, a breathtakingly scenic corridor located in the Wasatch Mountains of Utah, is a treasure trove of natural beauty and outdoor recreation. Just a short drive from Salt Lake City, this 15-mile-long canyon offers visitors a chance to immerse themselves in the serenity and splendor of Utah's rugged landscape. Known for its towering peaks, serene alpine lakes, and dense forests, Big Cottonwood Canyon is a year-round destination for nature lovers, hikers, skiers, and photographers.

In the winter, the canyon transforms into a world-class skiing and snowboarding destination, home to two of Utah's most beloved ski resorts: Brighton and Solitude. These resorts are celebrated for their diverse terrain, family-friendly atmosphere, and exceptional snow quality, attracting winter sports enthusiasts from all over the world. The canyon's high elevation and unique climate contribute to its legendary light, powdery snow, making it a paradise for those seeking the ultimate winter adventure.

As the snow melts and warmer weather prevails, Big Cottonwood Canyon reveals a different kind of beauty. The canyon becomes a popular spot for hiking, rock climbing, fishing, and picnicking. Trails of varying difficulty levels lead adventurers to breathtaking vistas, secluded mountain lakes, and through wildflower-covered meadows. The Donut Falls Trail, leading to a unique waterfall that plunges through a donut-shaped hole in the rock, and the hike to Lake Blanche, with its stunning alpine views, are among the many must-do summer activities.

For those interested in the canyon's geology and history, the area offers insights into the forces that shaped the landscape millions of years ago, as well as the human history of the region, from Native American use to mining operations in the 19th and early 20th centuries.

Big Cottonwood Canyon is not just a destination; it's an experience that embodies the wild, untamed beauty of Utah. Whether blanketed in snow or basking in the summer sun, the canyon offers a peaceful retreat and an adventure playground for those seeking to reconnect with nature and explore the great outdoors.

12. Little Cottonwood Canyon

Little Cottonwood Canyon, nestled within the rugged Wasatch Range in Utah, is a captivating natural wonder that draws visitors from around the globe. This 15-mile long geological marvel, located a mere 20 miles from Salt Lake City, is famed for its steep walls, scenic vistas, and the renowned powder that makes it a winter sports paradise. Little Cottonwood Canyon is not just a destination; it's an invitation to explore the majestic beauty of Utah's landscape across all seasons.

In the winter, the canyon is transformed into a premier skiing destination, home to two of the world's most famous ski resorts: Alta and Snowbird. These resorts are celebrated for their exceptional snow quality, challenging terrain, and deep powder, attracting skiers of all levels. Alta, known for its skier-only slopes, offers a traditional skiing experience, while Snowbird provides a wide range of winter activities, including snowboarding. The accessibility of these resorts, combined with Utah's light, fluffy snow, makes Little Cottonwood Canyon a bucket-list destination for winter sports enthusiasts.

As the seasons change, the canyon sheds its blanket of snow to reveal lush greenery, wildflowers, and a network of trails that beckon hikers, climbers, and nature lovers. The canyon's summer beauty is equally breathtaking, with opportunities for rock climbing, bird watching, and exploring alpine lakes and streams. Hikes range from easy strolls, like the Temple Quarry Trail, to challenging treks such as the ascent to the summit of Mount Superior. The beauty of Cecret Lake, nestled high in the Albion Basin, is a highlight for many visitors, offering stunning views and a chance to witness local wildlife.

Little Cottonwood Canyon also holds historical significance, with remnants of its mining past visible along its trails. It served as a vital resource for the early settlers of Salt Lake Valley, with granite from its quarries used to construct the iconic Salt Lake Temple.

Whether blanketed in snow or basking in the alpine sun, Little Cottonwood Canyon offers a myriad of ways to experience the raw, untouched beauty of Utah. It's a place where adventure meets tranquility, inviting all who visit to immerse themselves in its enduring splendor.

13. Bell Canyon Trail

Bell Canyon Trail, located on the southeastern edge of the Salt Lake Valley in Utah, offers an invigorating escape into the wilderness, just a stone's throw from the urban sprawl. This popular hiking destination is renowned for its stunning natural beauty, challenging terrain, and the captivating Bell Canyon Reservoir and waterfalls that reward those who traverse its paths. The trail provides a perfect blend of accessibility and adventure, making it a favored spot for hikers, photographers, and nature enthusiasts alike.

The journey through Bell Canyon begins at the base of the Wasatch Mountains, where the trailhead introduces hikers to a moderate climb through a picturesque landscape. The path winds through scrub oak and pine, opening up to reveal expansive views of the Salt Lake Valley below. The sound of running water accompanies hikers as they ascend, enhancing the trail's serene ambiance.

One of the trail's highlights is the Lower Bell Canyon Reservoir, a tranquil spot ideal for picnicking or simply enjoying the peaceful surroundings. Beyond the reservoir, the trail becomes more strenuous, leading adventurers towards the spectacular Bell Canyon Waterfall. The sight and sound of the waterfall cascading down the rocky cliffside offer a refreshing reward for the uphill trek.

The Bell Canyon Trail continues beyond the waterfall, offering more experienced hikers the chance to explore further into the wilderness, with additional waterfalls and even more breathtaking vistas awaiting. The upper sections of the trail demand a higher level of fitness and preparation, but they promise unparalleled views and a deeper sense of solitude.

Throughout the seasons, Bell Canyon presents a dynamic landscape. Spring and summer months adorn the trail with wildflowers and lush greenery, while autumn brings a fiery display of fall foliage. Even in winter, the canyon retains its allure, with snow-covered paths and frozen waterfalls adding to its enchanting beauty.

14. The Living Planet Aquarium

The Living Planet Aquarium, situated in Draper, Utah, stands as a testament to the wonders of the natural world, offering visitors an immersive journey through diverse aquatic ecosystems. Since its opening, this state-of-the-art facility has captivated audiences with its expansive collection of marine and freshwater species, interactive exhibits, and dedication to conservation and education. It serves not only as a window to the underwater world but also as a center for environmental stewardship, inspiring visitors to appreciate and protect the planet's biodiversity.

Spanning several ecosystems, from the Utah deserts and wetlands to the vast oceans, The Living Planet Aquarium is home to over 4,000 animals from around 450 species. Each exhibit is meticulously designed to replicate natural habitats, providing a glimpse into the lives of its inhabitants and the ecological roles they play. One of the highlights is the Journey to South America exhibit, where a lush, tropical rainforest environment houses free-flying birds, curious otters, and majestic jaguars. The sounds of waterfalls and the sight of vibrant flora transport visitors to another world, far from the arid Utah landscape.

The Ocean Explorer exhibit offers another awe-inspiring experience with its 300,000-gallon shark tank, where guests can observe these magnificent creatures up close, along with stingrays and colorful fish species. The interactive touch pools, where visitors can gently touch stingrays and sea stars, further demystify the ocean's mysteries and encourage a hands-on approach to learning.

For families and young explorers, the aquarium's Discovery Zone provides an engaging learning environment with interactive displays, a water play area, and the opportunity to learn about various aquatic animals through up-close encounters. This space fosters curiosity and a deeper understanding of marine life, emphasizing the importance of conservation.

The Living Planet Aquarium does more than showcase the beauty of aquatic life; it plays an active role in conservation efforts, both locally and globally. Through research, rehabilitation programs, and educational initiatives, the aquarium is committed to making a difference in the health of our planet's waterways.

15. Thanksgiving Point

Thanksgiving Point, located in Lehi, Utah, is a sprawling complex that offers a unique blend of educational and recreational activities set against the backdrop of beautiful gardens and museums. This not-for-profit community resource was established in 1995 and has since grown into a cultural hub that attracts families, students, and visitors from all walks of life, seeking to explore, learn, and enjoy the diverse attractions it offers.

Spanning over 700 acres, Thanksgiving Point is home to several distinct venues, each providing its own unique experience. The Ashton Gardens feature 55 acres of stunning thematic gardens, including the largest manmade waterfall in the Western Hemisphere. These meticulously landscaped gardens invite visitors to stroll through a variety of flora and landscapes, offering a serene and breathtaking escape from the urban hustle.

The Museum of Ancient Life at Thanksgiving Point is one of the world's largest displays of mounted dinosaurs, providing an unparalleled journey back in time. Visitors can explore the earth's ancient inhabitants through interactive exhibits, educational displays, and hands-on activities that make prehistoric life accessible and engaging for all ages.

For those interested in agriculture and farm life, Farm Country gives guests a closer look at farm animals and modern farming operations. This attraction emphasizes the importance of agriculture in our daily lives and offers interactive experiences such as cow milking and pony rides, making it a favorite among younger visitors.

Thanksgiving Point also features the Butterfly Biosphere, an enchanting conservatory filled with hundreds of live butterflies from around the globe. This immersive exhibit allows visitors to walk among the butterflies, learn about their lifecycles, and understand the role they play in our ecosystems.

In addition to its permanent attractions, Thanksgiving Point hosts a variety of seasonal events, workshops, and educational programs designed to inspire curiosity and a love of learning. From the Tulip Festival in the spring to the Luminaria light display during the holiday season, there's always something new and exciting to experience.

16. Provo Canyon

Provo Canyon, a majestic natural corridor in the Wasatch Range of Utah, is a blend of scenic beauty and outdoor recreation that captivates both the adventurous spirit and those seeking tranquility. Carved by the Provo River and flanked by towering cliffs and verdant mountainsides, this canyon is a gateway to a world of exploration, offering a diverse array of activities throughout the year. Its proximity to Provo and Orem makes it an accessible retreat for locals and visitors alike, looking to immerse themselves in Utah's natural splendor.

One of the canyon's most iconic features is Bridal Veil Falls, a stunning 607-foot waterfall that cascades into the Provo River. The falls are easily accessible, making them a popular spot for families and photographers eager to capture the beauty of this natural wonder. In the warmer months, the base of the falls becomes a cool, misty haven for picnickers and those simply wishing to bask in the majesty of the waterfall.

Provo Canyon is also renowned for its extensive trail network, catering to hikers, bikers, and runners of all skill levels. The Provo River Parkway Trail, for instance, winds through the canyon, offering a paved path that follows the river's course, ideal for a leisurely stroll or a brisk bike ride. For the more adventurous, the canyon provides access to more strenuous hikes that lead to breathtaking vistas and secluded mountain lakes.

In addition to terrestrial adventures, the Provo River offers excellent opportunities for fishing, particularly for rainbow and brown trout, making it a favored destination for anglers. During the winter months, the canyon transforms into a snowy wonderland, with nearby Sundance Resort offering skiing and snowboarding against a spectacular alpine backdrop.

Beyond its natural attractions, Provo Canyon is steeped in history, with various points of interest that tell the story of the region's development and the people who have called it home. From Native American tribes to early Mormon settlers, the canyon's history adds a rich cultural layer to the natural beauty.

17. Stewart Falls

Stewart Falls stands as one of Utah's most picturesque and accessible natural attractions, captivating visitors with its cascading beauty against the backdrop of the rugged Wasatch Range. Located near Sundance Resort in Provo Canyon, this stunning two-tiered waterfall is a highlight for hikers and nature lovers exploring the area around Mount Timpanogos.

The falls plummet impressively over 200 feet in total, divided into two main sections that create a spectacular visual display. The upper tier elegantly spills over a rocky ledge before gathering and plunging again, forming the lower tier. This natural phenomenon is especially striking during the late spring and early summer months when the snowmelt from the higher elevations increases the water flow, adding to the majesty of the falls.

Access to Stewart Falls is facilitated by a well-maintained, approximately 3.5-mile round-trip trail that begins at the Aspen Grove Trailhead near Sundance Resort. The hike is rated as moderate, making it suitable for families and hikers of various skill levels. The trail winds through a beautiful forested area, opening up to wildflower meadows and offering occasional glimpses of Mount Timpanogos before culminating at the scenic overlook of the falls.

The area around Stewart Falls also provides an opportunity for visitors to engage with the natural environment more deeply, whether it's through photography, bird watching, or simply enjoying a quiet moment in the presence of such breathtaking scenery. The falls are not just a destination but a journey that offers a chance to appreciate the tranquility and beauty of Utah's mountainous landscape.

In addition to being a popular day hike, Stewart Falls serves as a reminder of the natural beauty that can be found within easy reach of Utah's urban areas. It embodies the serene and untamed spirit of the Wasatch Range, making it a must-visit location for anyone seeking to experience the awe-inspiring natural wonders of Utah.

18.   Sundance Mountain Resort

Sundance Mountain Resort, founded by Robert Redford in 1969, is nestled in the scenic North Fork Provo Canyon amidst the grandeur of Mount Timpanogos in Utah's Wasatch Range. This resort is more than just a skiing destination; it's a haven for artists, outdoor enthusiasts, and anyone seeking to connect with nature and experience the tranquil beauty of the mountains. Sundance stands out for its commitment to environmental preservation and its dedication to maintaining the natural balance of the canyon while offering a range of activities, accommodations, and cultural events.

In the winter, Sundance transforms into a world-class ski resort, offering a variety of slopes to accommodate skiers and snowboarders of all skill levels. With over 450 acres of skiable terrain, the resort provides a more intimate and uncrowded skiing experience compared to larger resorts, emphasizing quality over quantity. The snow-covered slopes, framed by towering evergreens and rugged mountain peaks, offer breathtaking views and an unmatched skiing experience.

Beyond skiing, Sundance offers a plethora of year-round activities. In the warmer months, the resort becomes a hub for outdoor adventure, including hiking, mountain biking, and zip-lining. The extensive trail system allows visitors to explore the diverse ecosystems of the Wasatch Range, from lush meadows filled with wildflowers to serene streams and waterfalls. The Full Moon Lift Rides offer a unique opportunity to witness the natural beauty of the mountains under the enchanting glow of the moon.

Sundance also prides itself on being a center for art and culture. The Sundance Institute, also founded by Redford, hosts the annual Sundance Film Festival, one of the premier independent film festivals in the world. The resort itself features art studios, workshops, and galleries, fostering a creative community that draws artists and enthusiasts from around the globe.

Accommodations at Sundance range from rustic cabins to mountain homes and suites, all designed to blend seamlessly with the natural surroundings. Dining options at the resort celebrate the spirit of the West, offering dishes made with sustainably sourced ingredients.

19. American Fork Canyon

American Fork Canyon, cradled in the heart of the Wasatch Mountains in Utah, is a natural sanctuary known for its dramatic alpine landscapes, extensive outdoor recreation opportunities, and rich historical background. This canyon is not only a gateway to adventure for outdoor enthusiasts but also a place of profound natural beauty that appeals to visitors of all ages. With its towering cliffs, cascading waterfalls, and dense forests, American Fork Canyon offers a picturesque setting for a myriad of activities throughout the year.

The canyon is home to the Timpanogos Cave National Monument, a highlight for many visitors. This underground wonder features an intricate system of caves filled with stunning formations of stalactites, stalagmites, and helictites. Accessible via a steep but scenic hike, the cave tour provides a fascinating glimpse into the geological history and underground marvels of the area.

For those seeking outdoor adventures, American Fork Canyon offers ample opportunities for hiking, mountain biking, rock climbing, and fishing. The canyon's trail system caters to all skill levels, with paths leading to serene alpine lakes, such as Silver Lake Flat Reservoir, and offering breathtaking views of the surrounding peaks and valleys. Rock climbers flock to the canyon to test their skills on its granite walls, while anglers find solace along the banks of the American Fork River, known for its excellent trout fishing.

During the winter months, the canyon transforms into a snowy retreat, with areas for snowshoeing and backcountry skiing. The snow-capped landscape provides a tranquil backdrop for winter sports enthusiasts seeking solitude and natural beauty.

American Fork Canyon is also steeped in history, with remnants of its mining past visible along its trails and in the ghost towns that dot the area. These historical sites add an intriguing layer to the canyon's allure, inviting visitors to delve into the region's rich heritage.

With its natural splendor, array of recreational activities, and historical significance, American Fork Canyon stands as a testament to the wild, untamed beauty of Utah's landscape. It beckons visitors to explore its depths, offering a haven for adventure, reflection, and connection with nature.

20. Timpanogos Cave National Monument

Timpanogos Cave National Monument, nestled in the heart of the Wasatch Range in American Fork Canyon, Utah, is a subterranean wonderland that beckons adventurers and nature enthusiasts alike. This national monument, established to protect and preserve a remarkable cave system, offers visitors a unique opportunity to explore the intricate and fascinating world beneath the earth's surface. The caves are celebrated for their stunning formations of stalactites, stalagmites, helictites, and flowstone, showcasing the incredible artistry of nature's underground landscape.

The journey to Timpanogos Cave is an adventure in itself. Visitors embark on a steep, 1.5-mile hike up the canyon's side, gaining over 1,100 feet in elevation. This challenging but rewarding trek offers breathtaking views of American Fork Canyon and the surrounding Wasatch Mountains, providing a picturesque backdrop to the anticipation of the underground exploration ahead. The trail is not only a physical journey but also an opportunity to connect with the natural beauty and tranquility of the area.

Inside the cave, guided tours reveal a hidden world of mineral formations and colors. The cave system consists of three interconnected caves: Hansen Cave, Middle Cave, and Timpanogos Cave, each offering its own unique features and formations. The tour highlights include the Great Heart of Timpanogos, a massive heart-shaped stalactite, and the delicately balanced helictites that defy gravity in their intricate growth patterns. The caves' naturally cool temperatures offer a refreshing respite from the summer heat, making it a popular destination during the warmer months.

Timpanogos Cave National Monument is not only a site of natural beauty but also a center for education and conservation. The monument's staff are dedicated to preserving this fragile ecosystem while providing educational programs that highlight the geological processes that formed the caves, the importance of cave conservation, and the broader environmental significance of such natural formations.

21. Cascade Springs

Cascade Springs, nestled within the Uinta National Forest on the scenic Alpine Loop Scenic Byway near Midway, Utah, is a natural oasis of tranquility and beauty. This series of springs emerges from the Wasatch Mountains, feeding thousands of gallons of water each day into a series of cascading pools and terraces. The crystal-clear waters, lush vegetation, and accessible boardwalks make Cascade Springs a popular destination for nature lovers, families, and photographers seeking to capture the serene beauty of this unique natural feature.

The springs are accessible via a series of well-maintained boardwalks and paved paths that wind through the area, allowing visitors of all abilities to explore the environment with ease. These pathways offer various vantage points from which to view the waterfalls, springs, and vibrant aquatic plants that thrive in this moist, cool habitat. Informative signs along the trails provide insights into the area's ecology, hydrology, and history, enhancing the visitor experience with educational context.

The water at Cascade Springs is remarkably clear, allowing visitors to observe the underwater plants and small fish that inhabit the pools. The surrounding forest adds to the area's appeal, with a mix of aspen, maple, and conifer trees providing a colorful backdrop in the fall and a cool, shaded environment in the summer months. The area is also home to diverse wildlife, including deer, moose, and various bird species, making it an excellent spot for wildlife watching.

Cascade Springs is not just a summer destination; its beauty can be appreciated year-round. The changing seasons offer unique perspectives and experiences, from the lush greenery of summer to the spectacular autumn colors and the serene, snow-covered landscapes of winter.

Visiting Cascade Springs offers a peaceful retreat into nature, where the soothing sounds of cascading water and the beauty of the natural surroundings provide a respite from the hustle and bustle of daily life. It's a place where visitors can reconnect with the natural world, enjoy a leisurely walk, and appreciate the simple yet profound beauty of water in motion.

22. The Midway Ice Castles

The Midway Ice Castles, a breathtaking winter wonderland located in Midway, Utah, offers visitors an enchanting experience unlike any other. Created entirely from ice, this magical attraction is part of a larger, multi-location project that aims to bring fairy tales to life through the artful manipulation of water and cold. Nestled near the Wasatch Mountains, the Midway Ice Castles utilize tens of thousands of icicles hand-placed by professional ice artists to construct towering spires, glowing ice tunnels, cavernous archways, and intricate sculptures that sparkle under the winter sun and illuminate with ethereal lights by night.

Each year, the design of the Ice Castles varies, making every visit unique. The construction process begins in the late fall, with artists growing and harvesting icicles that are then meticulously placed to form the structures. Over time, the icicles fuse together, and with the continual addition of more icicles, the castles grow in size and complexity. This process continues throughout the winter, with the castles evolving and expanding until the warmer spring temperatures begin to melt the ice.

Visitors to the Midway Ice Castles can explore a variety of icy features, including winding mazes, grandiose thrones made of ice, and slides that offer a brisk ride. At night, LED lights embedded within the ice transform the castles into a dazzling display of color, creating a surreal and mesmerizing atmosphere. The experience is further enhanced by occasional fire performances and live music, adding to the mystical feel of the environment.

The Midway Ice Castles are not only a testament to human creativity and the beauty of nature but also a reminder of the fleeting nature of beauty itself. This temporary art installation invites visitors to step into a world of fantasy and wonder, providing a unique opportunity to marvel at the intricate beauty of ice and enjoy a moment of awe and inspiration in the heart of winter. It's a must-visit destination for families, couples, and anyone looking to experience the magic of winter in an unforgettable setting.

23. Heber Valley Railroad

The Heber Valley Railroad, affectionately known as the Heber Creeper to locals, is a historic heritage railroad that offers a journey back in time through the stunning landscapes of the Wasatch Mountains and along the shores of the Deer Creek Reservoir in Utah. This iconic railroad provides a unique opportunity for passengers to experience the charm of early 20th-century train travel while enjoying the breathtaking natural beauty of Heber Valley and the surrounding area.

Operating out of Heber City, the railroad features a variety of vintage locomotives and coaches that have been meticulously restored to their former glory. Throughout the year, the Heber Valley Railroad offers a range of themed excursions that cater to all ages and interests. From scenic daytime rides that showcase the majestic beauty of the changing seasons to special events like the Polar Express during the holiday season, Murder Mystery dinners, and the ever-popular Wizard's Train, each journey on the Heber Valley Railroad is designed to create lasting memories.

The train routes themselves are a highlight, winding through the valley, past rolling farmlands, and into the rugged beauty of Provo Canyon. Along the way, passengers are treated to views of Mount Timpanogos, cascading waterfalls, and the tranquil waters of Deer Creek Reservoir. The combination of the historic trains, the narrative of the area's history and folklore provided by the crew, and the spectacular natural scenery makes for an enchanting experience.

Moreover, the Heber Valley Railroad plays an important role in preserving Utah's rich railway heritage. It serves as a living museum, educating visitors about the vital role railroads played in the development of the American West. Whether you're a railroad enthusiast, history buff, or simply looking for a unique way to explore Utah's natural wonders, a ride on the Heber Valley Railroad promises an unforgettable adventure through the heart of the Wasatch Mountains.

24. The Homestead Crater

The Homestead Crater, located in Midway, Utah, is a natural geothermal spring that offers a one-of-a-kind experience to visitors. This remarkable natural wonder is housed within a 55-foot tall, beehive-shaped limestone rock that has been forming for over 10,000 years. The crater is the only warm scuba diving destination in the continental United States, making it a unique attraction for divers, swimmers, and those looking to soak in its mineral-rich waters.

The interior of the crater reveals a pool of warm, clear mineral water that stays at a constant temperature of 90-96 degrees Fahrenheit year-round. The water's buoyancy and warmth provide a relaxing and therapeutic experience, ideal for soothing sore muscles and joints. The crater's depth of 65 feet also makes it a popular site for scuba diving and snorkeling enthusiasts who are eager to explore its underwater wonders.

Access to the water is made easy by a tunnel that was carved through the rock in the 1990s, allowing visitors to enter without disturbing the crater's natural dome. Once inside, guests can choose to swim, snorkel, or even take a paddleboard yoga class on the tranquil waters. For those looking to dive deeper, scuba diving lessons and certification courses are offered, providing a rare opportunity to dive in such a unique and serene environment.

The Homestead Crater is not only a destination for water activities but also a geological curiosity. It offers an educational glimpse into the Earth's geothermal processes and the natural formation of hot springs. The site has been developed with respect for its natural beauty and ecological significance, ensuring that visitors can enjoy the crater's wonders without compromising its integrity.

Visiting the Homestead Crater is an immersive experience that blends adventure, relaxation, and education. It's a hidden gem in Utah's landscape, offering a peaceful escape into the warm embrace of nature's own hot tub, surrounded by the stunning scenery of the Wasatch Mountains.

25. Wasatch Mountain State Park

Wasatch Mountain State Park, nestled in the heart of Utah's magnificent Wasatch Range near the charming town of Midway, is a haven for outdoor enthusiasts and nature lovers. This expansive state park, covering nearly 23,000 acres, offers a diverse landscape of rolling hills, lush forests, and serene reservoirs, set against the backdrop of towering mountain peaks. It's a place where adventure and the tranquil beauty of nature coexist, providing visitors with endless opportunities to explore and enjoy the great outdoors.

The park boasts a wide array of recreational activities throughout the year. In the warmer months, hikers and mountain bikers take to the park's extensive network of trails, which wind through scenic vistas, alpine meadows, and dense aspen forests. The trails range from easy walks suitable for families to challenging treks that reward adventurers with breathtaking views of the Heber Valley and beyond. Golfers are drawn to Wasatch Mountain State Park for its two 18-hole courses, offering a unique golfing experience with stunning landscapes and elevation changes.

When winter blankets the park in snow, it transforms into a winter wonderland ideal for cross-country skiing, snowshoeing, and snowmobiling. The park's winter trails provide a peaceful retreat into the snow-covered forests, with the silence broken only by the crunch of snow underfoot and the occasional sighting of wildlife.

Fishing enthusiasts can enjoy the park's reservoirs, which are stocked with trout and provide a serene setting for a day spent by the water. The park also offers camping facilities, including tent and RV sites, as well as cabins, making it a perfect destination for an overnight stay amidst the natural beauty of the Wasatch Mountains.

Wasatch Mountain State Park is not just a destination for recreation; it's a place of conservation and education. The park serves as a gateway to understanding the delicate ecosystems of the Wasatch Range and the importance of preserving natural landscapes for future generations. Whether seeking adventure, relaxation, or a deeper connection with nature, Wasatch Mountain State Park offers a picturesque setting and a wealth of activities that make it a must-visit location in Utah.

26. The Pfeifferhorn

The Pfeifferhorn, often referred to as the "Little Matterhorn" due to its striking resemblance to its famous Swiss namesake, is one of the most iconic peaks in Utah's Wasatch Range. Standing at an elevation of 11,326 feet, it is the fifth highest peak in the range and offers one of the most rewarding and challenging alpine climbs in the area. Located in the Lone Peak Wilderness, the Pfeifferhorn showcases the rugged beauty of the Wasatch Mountains with its sharp, jagged ridgeline and panoramic views that stretch across central Utah.

The route to the summit of the Pfeifferhorn is a favorite among experienced hikers and mountaineers, known for its scenic beauty as well as its physical demands. The most common approach, via Red Pine Lake Trail, begins in the White Pine Trailhead in Little Cottonwood Canyon. The trail winds through dense forests, past serene alpine lakes, and across boulder fields before ascending the final steep ridge to the summit. This hike is a strenuous endeavor, covering roughly 9 miles round trip with significant elevation gain, but the effort is amply rewarded upon reaching the top. From the summit, climbers are greeted with breathtaking views of the surrounding alpine landscape, including Lone Peak to the south and the expansive Utah Valley to the west.

The Pfeifferhorn is not only a destination for those seeking the thrill of the climb but also a testament to the wild, untamed beauty of the Wasatch Range. The area is home to a diverse array of flora and fauna, including wildflowers that bloom in vibrant colors during the summer months, and wildlife such as mountain goats, moose, and various bird species. The climb and the surrounding wilderness area offer a profound sense of solitude and connection with nature, providing a stark contrast to the bustling city life just a short distance away.

For adventurers looking to experience the essence of the Wasatch Mountains, a climb to the summit of the Pfeifferhorn offers an unforgettable journey through some of Utah's most spectacular alpine scenery. It's a challenging but immensely rewarding excursion that embodies the adventurous spirit of the mountain west.

27. Alta Ski Area

Alta Ski Area, nestled at the top of Little Cottonwood Canyon in the Wasatch Mountains of Utah, is a revered destination among ski enthusiasts. With its slogan, "Ski Alta, Ski Pure," this area emphasizes a skiing experience that's both authentic and rooted in tradition. Established in 1938, Alta is among the oldest ski resorts in the United States and has maintained a strong commitment to preserving the pure joy of skiing in an ever-evolving winter sports industry.

Alta is renowned for its exceptional snow quality, receiving an average of over 500 inches of the light, fluffy snow known as "The Greatest Snow on Earth" annually. This abundance of snowfall, combined with the area's challenging terrain and breathtaking scenery, makes Alta a paradise for skiers of all levels, though it's particularly celebrated by advanced and expert skiers for its steep, off-piste runs and deep powder skiing opportunities.

Spanning over 2,600 acres, Alta's terrain is a mix of wide, groomed runs, challenging steeps, and open bowls, all serviced by a network of lifts designed to maximize time on the slopes. Unlike most ski resorts in North America, Alta remains a ski-only area, upholding a tradition that emphasizes the purity of skiing without the inclusion of snowboarding.

Beyond its slopes, Alta Ski Area fosters a close-knit community atmosphere, with a variety of lodging options from rustic lodges to comfortable condos, where guests can unwind and share their day's adventures. The area also offers ski schools, equipment rentals, and après-ski activities, ensuring that every visitor, from beginner to expert, can fully enjoy their time at Alta.

Alta's commitment to conservation is evident in its operations and the care taken to preserve the natural beauty of the surrounding environment. It's not just a ski resort; it's a sanctuary for those who love skiing and the mountains, offering an experience that's as much about connecting with nature as it is about enjoying the sport. For many, a trip to Alta Ski Area is not just a vacation; it's a pilgrimage to one of skiing's most sacred places.

28. Brighton Ski Resort

Nestled in the picturesque Wasatch Mountain Range of Utah, Brighton Ski Resort stands as a beacon for winter sports enthusiasts. Offering an array of activities for skiers and snowboarders alike, Brighton is renowned for its abundant snowfall, diverse terrain, and welcoming atmosphere.

With over 1,050 acres of skiable terrain, Brighton provides something for everyone, from beginners to seasoned experts. The resort boasts 66 runs, ranging from gentle slopes perfect for beginners to challenging black diamond trails that will test even the most skilled skiers. Additionally, Brighton is famous for its extensive terrain parks, featuring jumps, rails, and boxes, catering to freestyle skiers and snowboarders looking to showcase their skills.

One of the standout features of Brighton Ski Resort is its legendary powder snow. Situated in a prime location for snowfall, the resort receives an average of over 500 inches of snow each year, creating pristine conditions for skiing and snowboarding. This abundance of powder makes Brighton a haven for powder hounds seeking untouched slopes and exhilarating runs.

Beyond its exceptional skiing and snowboarding opportunities, Brighton offers a welcoming and laid-back atmosphere that sets it apart from larger, more commercialized resorts. Visitors can unwind in cozy lodges, enjoy delicious meals at on-mountain restaurants, and take in breathtaking views of the surrounding mountains.

For those seeking a break from the slopes, Brighton provides a range of other winter activities, including snowshoeing, cross-country skiing, and snowmobiling. Additionally, the resort hosts events and activities throughout the winter season, from live music performances to family-friendly festivals.

Whether you're an avid skier or snowboarder looking to tackle challenging terrain or a family seeking a memorable winter getaway, Brighton Ski Resort offers an unforgettable experience amidst the stunning beauty of the Wasatch Mountains.

29. Silver Lake

Tucked away in the heart of Utah's Big Cottonwood Canyon, Silver Lake offers a serene escape amidst breathtaking natural beauty. This pristine alpine lake, surrounded by towering pine trees and rugged peaks, serves as a tranquil haven for outdoor enthusiasts seeking solace in nature.

A popular destination for hiking, Silver Lake boasts a variety of scenic trails that cater to all skill levels. The Silver Lake Loop Trail, a leisurely 0.8-mile loop, offers easy access to stunning views of the lake and surrounding mountains, making it perfect for families and casual hikers. For more adventurous souls, the trail network extends to higher elevations, providing opportunities for longer treks and panoramic vistas.

In addition to hiking, Silver Lake is renowned for its excellent fishing opportunities. The lake is stocked with rainbow trout, providing anglers with the chance to reel in their catch amidst the tranquil surroundings.

Visitors to Silver Lake can also enjoy picnicking beside the water, birdwatching, or simply soaking in the serenity of nature. During the summer months, the area bursts to life with vibrant wildflowers, adding to the beauty of this idyllic mountain retreat.

Whether you're seeking outdoor adventure or simply a peaceful escape from the hustle and bustle of everyday life, Silver Lake offers a rejuvenating experience in one of Utah's most scenic settings.

30.   Solitude Mountain Resort

Nestled amid the pristine beauty of the Wasatch Mountains, Solitude Mountain Resort offers a tranquil retreat for outdoor enthusiasts year-round. With its uncrowded slopes, diverse terrain, and charming village atmosphere, Solitude provides an idyllic setting for skiing, snowboarding, and mountain adventures.

Solitude boasts over 1,200 acres of skiable terrain, ranging from gentle beginner slopes to challenging expert runs. The resort's layout is designed to minimize lift lines and congestion, allowing visitors to enjoy uninterrupted days on the slopes. With an average annual snowfall of over 500 inches, skiers and snowboarders can revel in the renowned Utah powder that blankets the mountain each winter.

In addition to its exceptional skiing and snowboarding, Solitude offers a variety of other winter activities to suit all interests. From snowshoeing and cross-country skiing to snowmobiling and ice skating, there's no shortage of ways to explore the winter wonderland surrounding the resort.

During the summer months, Solitude transforms into a haven for outdoor adventurers, with miles of hiking and mountain biking trails to explore. Visitors can immerse themselves in the beauty of the Wasatch Mountains, spotting wildlife, admiring wildflowers, and taking in panoramic views of the surrounding landscape.

After a day of adventure, guests can unwind in the resort's charming village, which features cozy lodges, inviting restaurants, and boutique shops. Whether savoring a gourmet meal, relaxing by the fire pit, or indulging in a spa treatment, Solitude offers the perfect blend of luxury and tranquility.

Whether you're seeking adrenaline-pumping thrills on the slopes or a peaceful retreat in nature, Solitude Mountain Resort promises an unforgettable mountain getaway amidst the stunning beauty of the Wasatch Mountains.

31. Donut Falls

Nestled within the rugged beauty of the Wasatch Mountains in Utah, Donut Falls stands as a hidden gem waiting to be discovered by outdoor enthusiasts and nature lovers alike. This enchanting waterfall, named for the distinctive circular hole through which water cascades, offers a unique and memorable adventure for visitors seeking to immerse themselves in Utah's stunning wilderness.

Accessible via a picturesque hiking trail, Donut Falls Trail winds through towering pine forests and rocky terrain, leading adventurers on a scenic journey to the waterfall's mesmerizing beauty. The trail, suitable for hikers of all skill levels, spans approximately 1.5 miles round trip, making it an ideal excursion for families and casual hikers.

As hikers approach the waterfall, they are greeted by the sight and sound of water cascading through the circular opening in the rock, creating a magical and serene atmosphere. During the warmer months, visitors can wade into the cool waters of the pool below the falls, offering a refreshing respite from the summer heat.

Beyond its natural beauty, Donut Falls also serves as a playground for outdoor exploration and photography. Adventurous souls can scramble over rocks to get a closer look at the waterfall, while photographers can capture stunning images of the cascading water framed by the surrounding wilderness.

Donut Falls epitomizes the raw beauty and tranquility of Utah's natural landscapes, offering visitors a chance to disconnect from the hustle and bustle of daily life and reconnect with the wonders of the natural world.

32. The Utah Olympic Park

Situated amidst the breathtaking scenery of Park City, Utah Olympic Park stands as a testament to the spirit of athleticism and the pursuit of excellence. Built for the 2002 Winter Olympics, this world-class facility continues to serve as a hub for winter sports enthusiasts and a living legacy of the Olympic Games.

The Utah Olympic Park offers a wide range of activities and attractions for visitors of all ages and interests. Thrill-seekers can experience the rush of adrenaline by taking a ride on the park's iconic bobsled track, where professional drivers guide guests on an exhilarating journey down the icy course at speeds reaching up to 70 miles per hour.

For those seeking a more grounded adventure, the park boasts a variety of other attractions, including zip lines, ropes courses, and a freestyle aerial training facility. Visitors can also explore interactive exhibits and displays that showcase the history and legacy of the Olympic Games, providing insight into the dedication and determination of athletes who have competed on the world stage.

In addition to its adrenaline-pumping activities, Utah Olympic Park serves as a training center for aspiring athletes, offering world-class facilities for athletes to hone their skills in sports such as ski jumping, Nordic combined, and freestyle skiing.

Whether you're a thrill-seeker looking for an adrenaline rush or a sports enthusiast eager to explore the legacy of the Olympic Games, Utah Olympic Park offers an unforgettable experience amidst the stunning beauty of Park City.

33. Park City

Nestled in the majestic Wasatch Mountains of Utah, Park City beckons visitors with its unique blend of historic charm and outdoor adventure. This vibrant mountain town, once a booming mining hub, has evolved into a premier destination for year-round recreation, culture, and entertainment.

Park City's historic Main Street serves as the heart of the town, lined with quaint shops, art galleries, and award-winning restaurants housed in beautifully preserved Victorian-era buildings. Visitors can stroll along the picturesque street, soaking in the atmosphere and admiring the town's rich history.

In addition to its historic charm, Park City offers a wealth of outdoor activities for adventurers of all ages and interests. During the winter months, the town transforms into a winter wonderland, with world-class skiing and snowboarding opportunities available at the nearby resorts of Park City Mountain and Deer Valley Resort.

In the summer, Park City's mountainous terrain becomes a playground for hiking, mountain biking, and outdoor exploration. Miles of scenic trails wind through pristine forests and meadows, offering breathtaking views of the surrounding mountains and valleys.

Park City also boasts a vibrant cultural scene, with festivals, concerts, and events held throughout the year. Visitors can immerse themselves in the town's artistic community, attending live performances, art exhibits, and film screenings that celebrate the diversity and creativity of Park City.

Whether you're seeking outdoor adventure, cultural experiences, or simply a peaceful retreat in the mountains, Park City offers something for everyone amidst its stunning natural beauty and rich heritage.

34. Deer Valley Resort

Nestled in the breathtaking Wasatch Mountains of Utah, Deer Valley Resort stands as a pinnacle of luxury skiing, offering an unparalleled experience for discerning winter sports enthusiasts. Renowned for its impeccable service, meticulously groomed slopes, and world-class amenities, Deer Valley embodies the essence of alpine elegance and adventure.

Spanning over 2,000 acres of pristine terrain, Deer Valley boasts a diverse range of ski runs catering to skiers and snowboarders of all levels, from gentle beginner slopes to challenging expert trails. With an average annual snowfall of over 300 inches and state-of-the-art snowmaking capabilities, the resort ensures optimal skiing conditions throughout the winter season.

One of the hallmarks of Deer Valley Resort is its commitment to providing guests with a first-class experience both on and off the slopes. From the moment visitors arrive, they are greeted with warm hospitality and attentive service, setting the stage for a memorable stay. The resort's luxurious lodges, elegant dining options, and exclusive amenities cater to every need and desire, ensuring a truly indulgent retreat in the mountains.

In addition to its exceptional skiing and snowboarding opportunities, Deer Valley offers a variety of other winter activities to enjoy, including snowshoeing, cross-country skiing, and horse-drawn sleigh rides. Guests can also relax and unwind at the resort's world-renowned spas, where they can indulge in rejuvenating treatments and massages after a day of outdoor adventure.

Beyond its winter offerings, Deer Valley transforms into a scenic playground for outdoor enthusiasts during the summer months. Visitors can explore miles of hiking and mountain biking trails, tee off at championship golf courses, or simply relax and take in the stunning mountain views.

With its blend of unparalleled luxury, world-class skiing, and picturesque mountain scenery, Deer Valley Resort offers an unforgettable alpine experience for those seeking the ultimate in mountain luxury and adventure.

35. Jordanelle State Park

Located just minutes from the vibrant town of Park City, Utah, Jordanelle State Park beckons visitors with its pristine reservoir, scenic landscapes, and abundant recreational opportunities. Whether you're seeking water-based activities, hiking and biking trails, or simply a peaceful escape amidst nature, Jordanelle offers something for everyone to enjoy.

At the heart of the park lies Jordanelle Reservoir, a sparkling oasis surrounded by rolling hills and towering mountains. Here, visitors can partake in a variety of water-based activities, including boating, fishing, paddleboarding, and swimming. With its clear blue waters and stunning mountain backdrop, Jordanelle Reservoir provides the perfect setting for a day of fun in the sun with family and friends.

In addition to its aquatic offerings, Jordanelle State Park boasts miles of scenic trails that wind through lush meadows, dense forests, and rugged terrain. Hikers and mountain bikers can explore the park's diverse landscapes, spotting wildlife, wildflowers, and panoramic views along the way. Popular trails include the Perimeter Trail, which offers a scenic loop around the reservoir, and the Rail Trail, a historic route that follows the path of an old railway line.

For those seeking a more laid-back experience, Jordanelle offers picnicking areas, playgrounds, and designated wildlife viewing areas where visitors can relax and soak in the natural beauty of the park. During the winter months, the park transforms into a snowy wonderland, offering opportunities for snowshoeing, cross-country skiing, and ice fishing.

With its stunning scenery, abundant recreational opportunities, and tranquil atmosphere, Jordanelle State Park provides the perfect escape for outdoor enthusiasts seeking to connect with nature and create lasting memories in Utah's great outdoors.

36. Mirror Lake

Nestled within the scenic Uinta Mountains of Utah, Mirror Lake stands as a pristine alpine gem, offering visitors a tranquil retreat amidst breathtaking natural beauty. Named for its glassy waters that perfectly reflect the surrounding mountains and forests, Mirror Lake provides a picturesque setting for outdoor adventure and exploration.

Accessible via the Mirror Lake Scenic Byway, one of Utah's most scenic drives, visitors are treated to panoramic views of towering peaks, dense forests, and crystal-clear lakes as they wind their way through the Uinta Mountains. The drive itself is a destination, offering countless opportunities for photography, wildlife viewing, and simply enjoying the serenity of nature.

Upon reaching Mirror Lake, visitors are greeted by the sight of its tranquil waters, which mirror the surrounding landscape like a perfectly polished mirror. The lake serves as a popular destination for fishing, with abundant populations of trout and other freshwater species inhabiting its depths. Anglers can cast their lines from the shore or rent a boat to explore the lake's hidden coves and fishing hotspots.

In addition to fishing, Mirror Lake offers a variety of other recreational activities to enjoy. Hikers can explore numerous trails that wind through the surrounding wilderness, ranging from easy strolls to challenging treks that lead to panoramic viewpoints and cascading waterfalls. During the summer months, visitors can also enjoy picnicking, camping, and wildlife viewing amidst the stunning beauty of the Uinta Mountains.

Mirror Lake is not just a destination; it's an experience that invites visitors to slow down, immerse themselves in nature, and appreciate the simple beauty of the world around them. Whether you're seeking outdoor adventure or simply a peaceful retreat in the mountains, Mirror Lake offers a serene escape from the hustle and bustle of everyday life.

37. King's Peak

As the highest peak in Utah, King's Peak stands as a majestic symbol of nature's grandeur and challenges adventurers to conquer its summit. Situated in the remote and rugged Uinta Mountains, King's Peak offers a thrilling and rewarding climbing experience for those seeking to test their skills and witness breathtaking vistas from the top.

Rising to an elevation of 13,534 feet (4,125 meters), King's Peak dominates the skyline of the Uinta Mountains, beckoning climbers with its imposing presence. The journey to the summit is not for the faint of heart, requiring careful planning, physical endurance, and a spirit of adventure.

The most popular route to King's Peak begins at the Henrys Fork Trailhead, where hikers embark on a challenging trek through alpine meadows, dense forests, and rugged terrain. Along the way, adventurers may encounter wildlife such as elk, deer, and mountain goats, adding to the allure of the wilderness experience.

As climbers ascend higher into the mountains, the landscape becomes increasingly dramatic, with towering peaks, cascading waterfalls, and expansive vistas unfolding before their eyes. The final push to the summit involves navigating steep slopes and rocky terrain, culminating in a triumphant arrival at the highest point in Utah.

From the summit of King's Peak, climbers are rewarded with panoramic views of the surrounding Uinta Mountains, as well as distant vistas stretching into neighboring states. On a clear day, it's possible to see for miles in every direction, offering a sense of awe and accomplishment that can only be found at high altitudes.

While reaching the summit of King's Peak is a challenging endeavor, the journey itself is filled with moments of wonder and beauty that make it truly unforgettable. Whether you're an experienced mountaineer or a novice adventurer looking to push your limits, King's Peak offers an exhilarating and awe-inspiring climbing experience that will leave a lasting impression.

38. Bear Lake

Nestled on the border between Utah and Idaho, Bear Lake is a sparkling gem of turquoise waters surrounded by lush forests and sandy beaches. Dubbed the "Caribbean of the Rockies" for its striking blue hues, Bear Lake offers visitors a serene escape amidst stunning natural beauty and a wealth of recreational opportunities.

The centerpiece of Bear Lake is its crystal-clear waters, which shimmer in shades of blue reminiscent of tropical seas. Whether you're swimming, boating, or simply relaxing on the shore, the lake's inviting waters provide the perfect backdrop for a day of fun and relaxation with family and friends.

Boating enthusiasts will delight in the opportunity to explore Bear Lake's expansive waters, which stretch over 20 miles in length and offer ample space for sailing, water skiing, and jet skiing. Anglers will also find plenty to love about Bear Lake, with abundant populations of trout, whitefish, and other freshwater species inhabiting its depths.

In addition to its water-based activities, Bear Lake boasts a variety of other recreational opportunities for visitors to enjoy. Hiking and biking trails wind through the surrounding forests and meadows, offering scenic vistas and opportunities for wildlife viewing. During the winter months, the area transforms into a snowy wonderland, with opportunities for snowmobiling, cross-country skiing, and ice fishing.

Bear Lake is also known for its vibrant community and rich cultural heritage, with events and festivals held throughout the year that celebrate the area's history, traditions, and natural beauty. From summer fireworks displays to winter carnivals, there's always something exciting happening at Bear Lake.

Whether you're seeking outdoor adventure, relaxation, or simply a scenic retreat in nature, Bear Lake offers something for everyone to enjoy amidst its stunning turquoise waters and picturesque surroundings.

39. Uinta Mountains

The Uinta Mountains, located in northeastern Utah, stand as a wilderness wonderland waiting to be explored. Spanning over 400,000 acres of pristine wilderness, this rugged and remote mountain range offers outdoor enthusiasts a paradise of alpine lakes, towering peaks, and breathtaking landscapes.

One of the most striking features of the Uinta Mountains is its unique east-west orientation, which sets it apart from the north-south trending ranges typical of the Rocky Mountains. This geological anomaly results in a landscape characterized by rolling hills, deep valleys, and countless streams and rivers, creating a haven for outdoor adventure and exploration.

The Uinta Mountains are home to a diverse array of wildlife, including elk, deer, moose, black bears, and mountain lions, making it a popular destination for wildlife enthusiasts and photographers. Visitors may also encounter rare species such as bighorn sheep and Rocky Mountain goats, which inhabit the high alpine regions of the range.

The Uinta Mountains offer a wealth of recreational opportunities for outdoor enthusiasts of all interests and skill levels. Hiking trails crisscross the landscape, leading adventurers through lush forests, alpine meadows, and rugged terrain to stunning vistas and hidden gems. Popular destinations include Kings Peak, the highest peak in Utah, and Mirror Lake, a scenic alpine lake renowned for its tranquil beauty.

In addition to hiking, the Uinta Mountains offer opportunities for fishing, camping, backpacking, rock climbing, and wildlife viewing. During the winter months, the area transforms into a snowy wonderland, with opportunities for snowshoeing, cross-country skiing, and snowmobiling.

Whether you're seeking a challenging backcountry adventure or a peaceful retreat in nature, the Uinta Mountains offer endless opportunities for exploration and discovery amidst some of Utah's most stunning landscapes.

Basin and Ridge Region

1. The Spiral Jetty

Nestled on the northeastern shore of the Great Salt Lake in Utah, the Spiral Jetty is a mesmerizing work of land art that captivates visitors with its striking beauty and thought-provoking design. Created in 1970 by renowned artist Robert Smithson, the Spiral Jetty is a testament to the intersection of art and nature, offering a unique and immersive experience in one of Utah's most scenic landscapes.

Constructed entirely from mud, salt crystals, and basalt rocks gathered from the surrounding area, the Spiral Jetty forms a massive, 1,500-foot-long coil that spirals counterclockwise into the lake. The artwork's location on the shores of the Great Salt Lake lends it an ever-changing character, as the water levels fluctuate and the colors of the landscape shift with the seasons.

Visitors to the Spiral Jetty are invited to walk along its winding path, tracing the contours of the earth and immersing themselves in the artwork's vast and otherworldly presence. As they follow the spiral's gradual descent into the water, they are enveloped by the sights, sounds, and smells of the surrounding landscape, creating a deeply immersive and contemplative experience.

Beyond its aesthetic appeal, the Spiral Jetty serves as a symbol of humanity's relationship with the natural world, prompting viewers to consider the interconnectedness of art, landscape, and environment. Its remote location and minimalistic design evoke a sense of solitude and introspection, inviting visitors to reflect on their place within the broader tapestry of nature.

Over the years, the Spiral Jetty has become an iconic landmark and a destination for art enthusiasts, nature lovers, and adventurers alike. Its remote location and ever-changing appearance make it a truly unique and unforgettable destination, offering a glimpse into the intersection of art and nature in one of Utah's most breathtaking landscapes.

2. Great Salt Lake

Spanning over 1,700 square miles, the Great Salt Lake is the largest saltwater lake in the Western Hemisphere and one of Utah's most iconic natural wonders. Nestled between the Wasatch Range to the east and the Stansbury and Oquirrh Mountains to the west, the lake's vast expanse and unique geological features make it a captivating destination for visitors from around the world.

The Great Salt Lake is renowned for its high salinity, which gives rise to its distinctive name and contributes to its unique ecosystem. The lake's waters are so saline that they support only a few species of brine shrimp and algae, making it inhospitable to most aquatic life. Despite this, the lake provides vital habitat for millions of migratory birds, including pelicans, gulls, and shorebirds, making it a haven for birdwatchers and wildlife enthusiasts.

In addition to its ecological significance, the Great Salt Lake offers a wealth of recreational opportunities for visitors to enjoy. Popular activities include swimming, boating, and picnicking at Antelope Island State Park, which boasts sandy beaches, scenic hiking trails, and stunning views of the surrounding mountains.

The Great Salt Lake's unique beauty and ecological diversity make it a must-see destination for anyone visiting Utah. Whether you're exploring its shores, marveling at its vibrant sunsets, or simply soaking in the serenity of its surroundings, the Great Salt Lake offers a truly unforgettable experience in the heart of the American West.

3. Antelope Island State Park

Located within the Great Salt Lake, Antelope Island State Park is a tranquil oasis of natural beauty and outdoor adventure. Spanning over 28,000 acres, the park offers visitors a pristine wilderness setting characterized by sandy beaches, rugged mountains, and abundant wildlife, making it a popular destination for hiking, camping, and wildlife viewing.

One of the highlights of Antelope Island State Park is its diverse array of wildlife, including bison, pronghorn antelope, mule deer, and bighorn sheep. Visitors can observe these iconic species in their natural habitat as they roam freely across the island's grassy plains and rocky hillsides. Birdwatchers will also delight in the park's resident and migratory bird populations, which include eagles, hawks, pelicans, and shorebirds.

In addition to its wildlife, Antelope Island State Park offers a variety of recreational activities for visitors to enjoy. Hiking trails wind through the park's scenic landscapes, offering stunning views of the surrounding mountains and Great Salt Lake. Cyclists can explore the island's network of paved and unpaved roads, while water enthusiasts can swim, boat, and kayak in the lake's tranquil waters.

Antelope Island State Park is also home to historical and cultural sites that offer insight into the island's rich history and heritage. Visitors can explore the Fielding Garr Ranch, one of the oldest and best-preserved pioneer homesteads in Utah, or visit the visitor center to learn about the island's geology, ecology, and wildlife.

Whether you're seeking outdoor adventure, wildlife viewing, or simply a peaceful retreat in nature, Antelope Island State Park offers something for everyone to enjoy amidst the stunning beauty of the Great Salt Lake.

4. Stansbury Island

Situated in the heart of the Great Salt Lake, Stansbury Island offers a rugged and remote escape for adventurers seeking to explore Utah's unique natural landscapes. Despite its proximity to the bustling city of Salt Lake City, Stansbury Island remains relatively untouched by development, making it a pristine wilderness destination for hiking, camping, and outdoor exploration.

Spanning over 30 square miles, Stansbury Island is the second-largest island in the Great Salt Lake and boasts a diverse range of landscapes, from rocky cliffs and sandy beaches to rolling hills and sagebrush flats. The island's rugged terrain provides ample opportunities for hiking and exploration, with miles of scenic trails winding through its scenic landscapes.

One of the highlights of Stansbury Island is its panoramic views of the Great Salt Lake and surrounding mountains. Visitors can hike to the island's highest point, Stansbury Peak, which offers breathtaking vistas of the lake, as well as the Wasatch Range to the east and the Stansbury Mountains to the west.

In addition to its natural beauty, Stansbury Island is home to a variety of wildlife, including mule deer, bighorn sheep, and a wide array of bird species. Birdwatchers will delight in the opportunity to spot eagles, hawks, herons, and other birdlife as they explore the island's diverse habitats.

Stansbury Island also offers excellent opportunities for camping, with several primitive campsites located along its shores. Campers can pitch their tents amidst the island's stunning scenery, enjoy a night under the stars, and fall asleep to the gentle sound of waves lapping against the shore.

Whether you're hiking, camping, or simply enjoying the serenity of nature, Stansbury Island offers a pristine wilderness experience that's just a short drive from the city. With its rugged beauty and remote location, it's no wonder that Stansbury Island remains a hidden gem on the Great Salt Lake.

5. Bonneville Salt Flats

Stretching for miles across the western deserts of Utah, the Bonneville Salt Flats are a surreal landscape of shimmering white salt crusts, where the horizon seems to stretch on forever and the sky meets the earth in an endless expanse of blue. Renowned for its flat, hard-packed surface, the salt flats have become a legendary destination for speed enthusiasts, as well as a captivating natural wonder for travelers from around the world.

Formed thousands of years ago by the evaporation of ancient Lake Bonneville, the salt flats cover an area of over 30,000 acres and are one of the largest salt pans in the world. The vast expanse of white salt crusts creates a mesmerizing visual spectacle, particularly during sunrise and sunset when the landscape is bathed in hues of pink, orange, and gold.

The Bonneville Salt Flats are perhaps best known for their association with land speed racing, with numerous world records for land speed set on its iconic surface. Each year, speed enthusiasts from around the globe gather at the flats to test the limits of their vehicles and push the boundaries of human achievement.

In addition to its association with speed racing, the Bonneville Salt Flats offer a unique and otherworldly setting for photography, film, and exploration. Visitors can walk out onto the salt crusts, marveling at the vastness of the landscape and the surreal beauty of their surroundings.

Despite its harsh and inhospitable environment, the Bonneville Salt Flats are teeming with life, with numerous species of birds, insects, and plants adapted to survive in the salty soil. Birdwatchers will delight in the opportunity to spot shorebirds, waterfowl, and migratory species as they traverse the salt flats.

Whether you're a speed enthusiast looking to break records or a traveler seeking a one-of-a-kind natural wonder, the Bonneville Salt Flats offer an unforgettable experience amidst the stunning beauty of Utah's western deserts.

6. Silver Island Mountains Backcountry Byway

Situated in the remote western deserts of Utah, the Silver Island Mountains Backcountry Byway offers travelers a scenic and adventurous journey through some of the state's most rugged and untamed landscapes. Named for the striking silver-colored peaks that dominate the horizon, this 45-mile dirt road traverses the heart of the Silver Island Mountains, offering stunning views, fascinating geology, and opportunities for outdoor exploration.

The Silver Island Mountains Backcountry Byway begins near the shores of the Great Salt Lake and winds its way through a diverse array of desert landscapes, from rolling sand dunes and rocky canyons to towering mountain peaks and sweeping vistas. Along the way, travelers are treated to panoramic views of the surrounding desert wilderness, as well as glimpses of wildlife such as bighorn sheep, pronghorn antelope, and golden eagles.

One of the highlights of the byway is its geological diversity, with rock formations dating back millions of years and offering insights into the region's ancient history. Travelers can stop at scenic viewpoints and interpretive sites to learn about the area's unique geology, including its volcanic origins, fossilized remains, and eroded rock formations.

In addition to its geological wonders, the Silver Island Mountains Backcountry Byway offers opportunities for outdoor recreation and adventure. Hiking trails wind through the desert landscape, offering opportunities to explore hidden canyons, discover ancient rock art, and marvel at the beauty of desert wildflowers in bloom.

Camping is also popular along the byway, with several primitive campsites located along its route. Campers can pitch their tents beneath the stars, enjoy a night by the campfire, and fall asleep to the sound of coyotes howling in the distance.

Whether you're seeking scenic beauty, geological wonders, or outdoor adventure, the Silver Island Mountains Backcountry Byway offers a truly unforgettable journey through some of Utah's most stunning and remote landscapes.

7. Utah Motorsports Campus

Located in Tooele, Utah, the Utah Motorsports Campus stands as a premier destination for motorsports enthusiasts and thrill-seekers alike. This state-of-the-art facility offers a wide range of motorsports activities and events, making it a hub of excitement and adrenaline for visitors of all ages.

The Utah Motorsports Campus features a variety of world-class racing facilities, including a 2.2-mile road course, a 0.9-mile karting track, and a 0.7-mile autocross course. These versatile tracks provide opportunities for amateur and professional racers alike to test their skills and push the limits of speed and performance.

In addition to its racing facilities, the Utah Motorsports Campus offers a range of other motorsports activities and events throughout the year. From high-performance driving schools and track days to professional racing events and motorcycle races, there's always something exciting happening at the campus.

One of the highlights of the Utah Motorsports Campus is its commitment to safety and accessibility, with state-of-the-art facilities and professional staff dedicated to providing a safe and enjoyable experience for all visitors. Whether you're a seasoned racer or a novice driver, the campus offers programs and services tailored to your skill level and interests.

Beyond its motorsports activities, the Utah Motorsports Campus also serves as a venue for corporate events, team-building activities, and private functions. With its scenic backdrop and world-class amenities, the campus provides the perfect setting for business meetings, conferences, and social gatherings.

Whether you're a motorsports enthusiast looking to test your skills on the track or a spectator eager to witness thrilling racing action, the Utah Motorsports Campus offers an unforgettable experience in the heart of Tooele.

8. Tooele Valley Railroad Museum

Nestled in the picturesque town of Tooele, Utah, the Tooele Valley Railroad Museum offers visitors a glimpse into the rich history of railroading in the American West. Housed in a historic train depot dating back to the early 20th century, the museum showcases a fascinating collection of artifacts, exhibits, and memorabilia that celebrate the impact of railroads on the development of Utah and the surrounding region.

The Tooele Valley Railroad Museum traces its origins to the Tooele Valley Railway, a short-line railroad that served the mining and industrial communities of Tooele County from the late 19th century to the mid-20th century. The museum's exhibits explore the history of the railway, highlighting its role in transporting minerals, goods, and passengers throughout the region.

Visitors to the Tooele Valley Railroad Museum can explore a variety of indoor and outdoor exhibits, including historic locomotives, railroad cars, and equipment. Highlights of the museum's collection include a vintage steam locomotive, a caboose, and a variety of railroad artifacts and memorabilia dating back to the golden age of railroading.

In addition to its exhibits, the Tooele Valley Railroad Museum offers a variety of educational programs, events, and activities for visitors of all ages. From guided tours and interpretive programs to special events such as train rides and model railroad displays, there's always something exciting happening at the museum.

The Tooele Valley Railroad Museum is also home to a dedicated team of volunteers and historians who are passionate about preserving Utah's railroad heritage and sharing it with future generations. Their efforts ensure that the museum remains a vibrant and engaging destination for visitors seeking to learn about the history of railroading in the American West.

Whether you're a railroad enthusiast, a history buff, or simply curious about Utah's rich railroad heritage, the Tooele Valley Railroad Museum offers a fascinating journey through the past and a unique glimpse into the role of railroads in shaping the landscape and culture of the American West.

9. Deseret Peak Wilderness

Situated in the rugged mountains of Tooele County, Utah, the Deseret Peak Wilderness offers visitors a pristine and remote wilderness experience amidst stunning alpine landscapes and breathtaking vistas. Spanning over 20,000 acres of wilderness, this protected area is a haven for outdoor enthusiasts seeking solitude, adventure, and natural beauty.

The Deseret Peak Wilderness is named for its towering centerpiece, Deseret Peak, which rises to an elevation of 11,031 feet (3,362 meters) and offers panoramic views of the surrounding mountains and valleys. The peak serves as a popular destination for hikers and backpackers, who can explore a network of trails that wind through alpine meadows, dense forests, and rugged terrain.

One of the highlights of the Deseret Peak Wilderness is its diverse array of ecosystems and habitats, which support a wide range of wildlife species. Visitors may encounter mule deer, elk, mountain goats, and a variety of bird species as they explore the wilderness, making it a popular destination for wildlife viewing and photography.

In addition to its hiking opportunities, the Deseret Peak Wilderness offers a variety of other outdoor activities for visitors to enjoy. Backpacking, camping, fishing, and horseback riding are all popular pursuits, allowing visitors to immerse themselves in the natural beauty of the wilderness and experience the tranquility of the mountain landscape.

Despite its remote location, the Deseret Peak Wilderness is easily accessible from nearby towns such as Tooele and Salt Lake City, making it a convenient destination for day trips, weekend getaways, and extended wilderness adventures. Whether you're seeking a challenging hike to the summit of Deseret Peak or a leisurely stroll through alpine meadows, the wilderness offers something for outdoor enthusiasts of all interests and abilities.

As a designated wilderness area, the Deseret Peak Wilderness is managed to preserve its natural and scenic values, ensuring that future generations can continue to enjoy its beauty and solitude for years to come.

10. Pony Express Trail

The Pony Express Trail traces a historic route that played a pivotal role in shaping the American West during the mid-19th century. Stretching over 1,900 miles from Missouri to California, this legendary trail was once a lifeline for communication and transportation, connecting the eastern and western United States in an era before the transcontinental railroad.

The Pony Express Trail originated in St. Joseph, Missouri, where it began its journey westward through the heart of the American frontier. Riders would carry mail and messages across vast stretches of wilderness, traversing rugged terrain, hostile landscapes, and unpredictable weather conditions in their quest to deliver the mail in record time.

One of the most iconic segments of the Pony Express Trail passes through the deserts and mountains of Utah, where riders faced some of the most challenging and treacherous conditions of their journey. The trail winds through remote and rugged landscapes, crossing expansive deserts, towering mountain ranges, and winding canyons as it makes its way towards the California coast.

Today, the Pony Express Trail offers visitors a chance to step back in time and experience the rugged beauty and pioneering spirit of the American West. Numerous historic sites and landmarks along the trail provide insights into the trail's storied past, including original Pony Express stations, trail markers, and interpretive exhibits.

One of the highlights of the Pony Express Trail in Utah is Simpson Springs, a historic watering hole and rest stop that served as a crucial outpost for Pony Express riders and travelers alike. Visitors can explore the remains of the original station, learn about the trail's history, and imagine what life was like for the brave riders who once traversed this rugged wilderness.

Whether you're a history buff, an outdoor enthusiast, or simply curious about the legacy of the American West, the Pony Express Trail offers a fascinating journey through time and a unique glimpse into the pioneering spirit that shaped the landscape and culture of the western United States.

11. Eagle Mountain

Nestled in the foothills of the Oquirrh Mountains in Utah County, Eagle Mountain is a rapidly growing community that embodies the spirit of the modern American frontier. Once a remote and sparsely populated area, Eagle Mountain has experienced significant growth and development in recent years, attracting residents and visitors with its scenic beauty, outdoor recreation opportunities, and vibrant community spirit.

Eagle Mountain is home to a diverse range of outdoor activities and attractions, making it a popular destination for outdoor enthusiasts and nature lovers. The area boasts miles of hiking and biking trails that wind through scenic landscapes, offering stunning views of the surrounding mountains and valleys. In addition to its trails, Eagle Mountain is also home to numerous parks, playgrounds, and recreational facilities, providing opportunities for outdoor adventure and relaxation for residents and visitors of all ages.

In addition to its outdoor amenities, Eagle Mountain offers a variety of community events and activities that celebrate its rich heritage and vibrant culture. From farmers markets and festivals to concerts and parades, there's always something happening in Eagle Mountain, making it a lively and dynamic place to live and visit.

Despite its rapid growth and development, Eagle Mountain remains committed to preserving its natural beauty and small-town charm. The city's master-planned communities are designed to blend seamlessly with the surrounding landscape, while its parks and open spaces are carefully maintained to protect the area's ecological diversity and wildlife habitat.

Whether you're seeking outdoor adventure, community spirit, or simply a peaceful retreat in nature, Eagle Mountain offers something for everyone to enjoy amidst the stunning beauty of Utah's modern frontier.

12. Utah Lake State Park

Utah Lake State Park is a picturesque destination nestled along the shores of Utah's largest freshwater lake. Situated in the heart of Utah Valley, the park offers visitors a wide range of outdoor recreational activities, including boating, fishing, swimming, and picnicking, making it a popular destination for families, anglers, and outdoor enthusiasts.

Utah Lake is renowned for its scenic beauty and diverse ecosystems, which support a rich variety of wildlife and plant species. The lake's expansive waters provide ample opportunities for boating and water sports, with boat ramps and marinas located throughout the park for easy access to the water.

Fishing is another popular activity at Utah Lake, with abundant populations of bass, trout, catfish, and other freshwater species inhabiting its waters. Anglers can cast their lines from shore or venture out onto the lake in search of the perfect fishing spot, while families can enjoy picnicking and swimming at designated beach areas.

In addition to its outdoor recreational activities, Utah Lake State Park offers a variety of amenities and facilities for visitors to enjoy. The park features campgrounds, picnic areas, and pavilions for day-use and overnight stays, as well as hiking and biking trails that wind through scenic landscapes and offer stunning views of the lake and surrounding mountains.

Utah Lake State Park is also home to a visitor center and museum, where visitors can learn about the history, ecology, and recreational opportunities of the lake. Interactive exhibits, educational programs, and interpretive displays provide insights into the lake's cultural significance and ecological importance, making it a must-visit destination for anyone interested in Utah's natural history.

Whether you're boating, fishing, hiking, or simply enjoying a day at the beach, Utah Lake State Park offers endless opportunities for outdoor recreation and relaxation amidst the stunning beauty of Utah's largest freshwater lake.

13. Springville Museum of Art

Situated in the heart of Utah Valley, the Springville Museum of Art stands as a cultural oasis, showcasing a diverse collection of artworks that celebrate the beauty, diversity, and creativity of the American West. Founded in 1937, the museum has earned a reputation as one of Utah's premier art institutions, attracting visitors from near and far with its world-class exhibits, educational programs, and community events.

The Springville Museum of Art is home to an extensive collection of American art, with a particular emphasis on works that capture the spirit and heritage of the western United States. The museum's permanent collection includes paintings, sculptures, and other works of art by renowned artists such as Maynard Dixon, LeConte Stewart, and Minerva Teichert, as well as contemporary artists working in a variety of mediums.

In addition to its permanent collection, the Springville Museum of Art hosts a rotating schedule of temporary exhibits, featuring works by local, national, and international artists. These exhibits explore a wide range of themes, styles, and artistic movements, providing visitors with opportunities to engage with new ideas, perspectives, and creative expressions.

The Springville Museum of Art also offers a variety of educational programs and outreach initiatives designed to inspire and engage audiences of all ages. From guided tours and hands-on art workshops to lectures, concerts, and film screenings, there's always something happening at the museum to spark curiosity, foster creativity, and promote lifelong learning.

The museum's picturesque setting, nestled against the backdrop of the Wasatch Mountains, adds to its charm and allure, providing visitors with a tranquil and inspiring environment in which to explore, learn, and connect with art and culture. Whether you're a seasoned art enthusiast or simply curious about the creative spirit of the American West, the Springville Museum of Art offers a rich and rewarding experience that's sure to leave a lasting impression.

14. Nebo Loop National Scenic Byway

The Nebo Loop National Scenic Byway offers travelers a breathtaking journey through some of Utah's most stunning and diverse landscapes, from towering mountain peaks and lush forests to rolling hillsides and rugged canyons. Stretching over 38 miles through the Uinta National Forest, this scenic byway provides unparalleled opportunities for outdoor recreation, wildlife viewing, and scenic photography, making it a must-see destination for anyone exploring the American West.

The Nebo Loop National Scenic Byway begins in Payson Canyon and winds its way through the rugged terrain of the Wasatch Mountains, offering panoramic views of the surrounding valleys and mountains. Along the way, travelers can explore a variety of recreational areas, hiking trails, and scenic overlooks, each offering its own unique perspective on the beauty and diversity of the landscape.

One of the highlights of the Nebo Loop National Scenic Byway is the opportunity to witness the changing seasons in all their glory. In the spring, the mountainsides burst into bloom with wildflowers, while the summer months bring lush green forests and cascading waterfalls. In the fall, the hillsides are ablaze with vibrant autumn colors, providing a stunning backdrop for scenic drives and outdoor adventures. And in the winter, the landscape is transformed into a winter wonderland, with snow-capped peaks and frost-covered trees creating a magical atmosphere.

In addition to its scenic beauty, the Nebo Loop National Scenic Byway is home to a variety of recreational activities for visitors to enjoy. Hiking, picnicking, camping, and wildlife viewing are popular pursuits, allowing travelers to immerse themselves in the natural beauty and tranquility of the Uinta National Forest.

Whether you're driving the byway, hiking its trails, or simply stopping to admire the views, the Nebo Loop National Scenic Byway offers a truly unforgettable experience amidst the breathtaking beauty of Utah's backcountry.

15. Little Sahara Recreation Area

Located in the heart of the Great Basin Desert in central Utah, the Little Sahara Recreation Area offers visitors a unique and thrilling outdoor experience amidst towering sand dunes, rolling sagebrush flats, and expansive desert landscapes. Spanning over 60,000 acres, this popular recreation area is a haven for off-road enthusiasts, sandboarders, and outdoor adventurers seeking excitement and adventure in the desert.

The centerpiece of the Little Sahara Recreation Area is its vast expanse of sand dunes, which rise to heights of up to 700 feet above the surrounding desert floor. These towering dunes provide endless opportunities for off-road vehicle enthusiasts to explore, with miles of designated trails and open riding areas that cater to all skill levels and interests.

In addition to off-road vehicle riding, the Little Sahara Recreation Area offers a variety of other outdoor activities for visitors to enjoy. Sandboarding and sand sledding are popular pursuits, allowing thrill-seekers to glide down the dunes at exhilarating speeds and experience the rush of adrenaline that comes from conquering the desert sands.

The recreation area also boasts numerous campsites, picnic areas, and hiking trails, providing opportunities for visitors to relax, unwind, and soak in the beauty of the desert landscape. Whether you're camping under the stars, enjoying a scenic hike, or simply watching the sunset over the sand dunes, the Little Sahara Recreation Area offers a truly unforgettable experience in the heart of Utah's desert wilderness.

Despite its remote location, the Little Sahara Recreation Area is easily accessible from nearby towns such as Delta and Nephi, making it a popular destination for day trips, weekend getaways, and extended outdoor adventures. Whether you're seeking excitement, relaxation, or simply a connection with nature, the Little Sahara Recreation Area offers something for everyone to enjoy amidst the stunning beauty of Utah's desert playground.

16. Yuba State Park

Yuba State Park, nestled along the eastern shores of Yuba Reservoir in central Utah, offers visitors a scenic oasis of outdoor recreation and natural beauty. Spanning over 22,000 acres, this expansive park boasts sandy beaches, sparkling waters, and stunning desert landscapes, making it a popular destination for boating, fishing, camping, and picnicking.

Yuba Reservoir is the centerpiece of the park, providing ample opportunities for water-based recreation and relaxation. Boaters can explore the reservoir's calm waters, fish for bass, walleye, and catfish, or simply soak up the sun on the sandy beaches. The reservoir's clear waters are also ideal for swimming, paddleboarding, and kayaking, offering visitors a refreshing escape from the summer heat.

In addition to its water-based activities, Yuba State Park offers a variety of amenities and facilities for visitors to enjoy. The park features numerous campgrounds with tent and RV sites, as well as picnic areas, playgrounds, and volleyball courts. Hiking and biking trails wind through the park's scenic landscapes, providing opportunities for visitors to explore the area's diverse flora and fauna.

One of the highlights of Yuba State Park is its natural beauty and scenic vistas. The park's desert landscapes are dotted with sagebrush, juniper trees, and colorful wildflowers, providing a picturesque backdrop for outdoor adventures and wildlife viewing. Birdwatchers will delight in the opportunity to spot a variety of bird species, including bald eagles, pelicans, and waterfowl, that inhabit the park's wetlands and shoreline.

Whether you're seeking outdoor adventure, relaxation, or simply a day of fun in the sun, Yuba State Park offers something for everyone to enjoy amidst the stunning beauty of central Utah's desert wilderness.

17. Great Basin Museum

Located in the historic town of Brigham City, Utah, the Great Basin Museum offers visitors a fascinating glimpse into the history, culture, and heritage of northern Utah and the surrounding Great Basin region. Housed in a beautifully restored historic building, the museum features a diverse collection of artifacts, exhibits, and interactive displays that showcase the area's rich cultural heritage and pioneering spirit.

The Great Basin Museum's exhibits explore a wide range of themes and topics, from the early Native American inhabitants of the region to the arrival of European settlers and the development of agriculture, industry, and commerce in northern Utah. Visitors can learn about the area's geology, ecology, and natural resources, as well as its diverse cultural traditions and heritage.

One of the highlights of the Great Basin Museum is its extensive collection of artifacts, which includes Native American artifacts, pioneer tools and implements, historic photographs, and memorabilia from the region's agricultural and industrial past. Interactive exhibits and hands-on activities allow visitors to immerse themselves in the history and culture of northern Utah, making it a popular destination for families, students, and history enthusiasts alike.

In addition to its exhibits, the Great Basin Museum offers a variety of educational programs, events, and activities for visitors of all ages. From guided tours and workshops to lectures, concerts, and community festivals, there's always something happening at the museum to inspire curiosity, foster learning, and promote appreciation for the area's rich cultural heritage.

Whether you're a history buff, a culture vulture, or simply curious about the heritage of northern Utah, the Great Basin Museum offers a fascinating journey through time and a unique glimpse into the people, places, and events that have shaped the region's history and identity.

18. Territorial Statehouse State Park Museum

Situated in the heart of Fillmore, Utah, the Territorial Statehouse State Park Museum stands as a monument to Utah's political history and heritage. Housed in a beautifully restored historic building that once served as the seat of government for the Utah Territory, the museum offers visitors a fascinating glimpse into the state's territorial period and the events that shaped its early development.

The Territorial Statehouse State Park Museum is home to an extensive collection of artifacts, exhibits, and interactive displays that explore the political, social, and cultural history of Utah during the territorial period. Visitors can learn about the challenges and triumphs faced by early settlers, the debates and decisions that shaped territorial politics, and the struggles and sacrifices of those who helped to build the state we know today.

One of the highlights of the museum is its beautifully restored interior, which features period furnishings, historic documents, and artifacts that bring the territorial period to life. Visitors can explore the chambers of the territorial legislature, the governor's office, and the courtroom, gaining insights into the daily workings of government and the issues that dominated public discourse during this formative period in Utah's history.

In addition to its exhibits, the Territorial Statehouse State Park Museum offers a variety of educational programs, events, and activities for visitors of all ages. From guided tours and living history demonstrations to lectures, workshops, and special events, there's always something happening at the museum to engage, educate, and inspire.

Whether you're a history buff, a political junkie, or simply curious about Utah's past, the Territorial Statehouse State Park Museum offers a unique and immersive experience that's sure to leave a lasting impression. Come explore the halls of power, walk in the footsteps of early pioneers, and discover the stories and secrets of Utah's territorial period at this historic museum in the heart of Fillmore.

19. Fremont Indian State Park and Museum

Nestled in the scenic Clear Creek Canyon of central Utah, Fremont Indian State Park and Museum offers visitors a captivating journey into the ancient cultures of the Fremont people who inhabited the region over a thousand years ago. This archaeological treasure trove boasts an impressive collection of rock art, artifacts, and reconstructed dwellings, providing insights into the daily lives, traditions, and beliefs of these early inhabitants.

The centerpiece of Fremont Indian State Park is the museum, which showcases a wide range of exhibits that highlight the archaeological discoveries made within the park's boundaries. Visitors can explore interactive displays, view artifacts such as pottery, tools, and jewelry, and learn about the Fremont people's hunting, gathering, and farming practices through the ages.

One of the highlights of the park is its extensive collection of rock art, which includes petroglyphs and pictographs dating back thousands of years. These ancient artworks, etched and painted onto the sandstone cliffs and boulders of the canyon, offer glimpses into the spiritual beliefs, cultural practices, and daily life of the Fremont people, making them a fascinating subject of study and exploration.

In addition to its museum exhibits and rock art sites, Fremont Indian State Park offers a variety of outdoor recreational opportunities for visitors to enjoy. Hiking trails wind through the scenic canyon landscape, offering stunning views of the surrounding mountains and valleys, while picnic areas provide opportunities for relaxation and enjoyment amidst the beauty of nature.

Whether you're a history buff, an outdoor enthusiast, or simply curious about the ancient cultures of Utah, Fremont Indian State Park and Museum offers a unique and immersive experience that's sure to leave a lasting impression.

20. Sevier Lake

Sevier Lake, located in the remote desert of western Utah, is a unique and fascinating destination for visitors seeking to explore the beauty and solitude of Utah's desert landscapes. This vast, shallow lakebed, situated at the bottom of a closed basin, offers visitors stunning views of the surrounding desert terrain, as well as opportunities for outdoor recreation, wildlife viewing, and photography.

Although Sevier Lake is often dry or nearly dry, especially during the summer months, it still supports a diverse array of wildlife and plant species adapted to its harsh desert environment. Birdwatchers will delight in the opportunity to spot migratory birds such as shorebirds, waterfowl, and wading birds that frequent the lakebed during the spring and fall migration seasons.

In addition to its wildlife, Sevier Lake offers visitors a chance to explore the unique geology and natural features of Utah's desert landscape. The lakebed is dotted with salt flats, sand dunes, and ancient shoreline terraces, providing a fascinating glimpse into the area's geological history and evolution over time.

Whether you're hiking, birdwatching, or simply enjoying the solitude of the desert, Sevier Lake offers a unique and unforgettable experience amidst the stunning beauty of Utah's desert wilderness.

21. Notch Peak

Notch Peak, located in the remote western desert of Utah, is a towering limestone cliff that rises over 2,000 feet above the surrounding desert floor, making it one of the tallest cliffs in North America. This dramatic geological feature offers visitors stunning views of the surrounding desert landscape, as well as opportunities for hiking, rock climbing, and photography.

The sheer magnitude of Notch Peak's towering cliffs and rugged terrain makes it a popular destination for outdoor enthusiasts seeking adventure and exploration in Utah's western desert. Hiking trails wind through the surrounding canyons and washes, offering visitors opportunities to explore the area's unique geology, flora, and fauna.

Rock climbers flock to Notch Peak to test their skills on its challenging limestone cliffs, which offer a variety of routes and challenges for climbers of all experience levels. From easy scrambles to technical climbs, there's something for everyone to enjoy amidst the towering majesty of Notch Peak.

Whether you're hiking, climbing, or simply admiring the stunning beauty of Utah's western desert, Notch Peak offers a truly unforgettable experience that's sure to leave a lasting impression.

22. Crystal Ball Cave

Crystal Ball Cave, located in the remote desert of western Utah, is a hidden gem waiting to be explored by adventurous spelunkers and geology enthusiasts. This fascinating limestone cave boasts an otherworldly beauty, with its intricate formations, sparkling crystals, and mysterious underground chambers offering visitors a glimpse into the earth's ancient past.

The cave's most notable feature is its abundance of crystal formations, including stalactites, stalagmites, and helictites, which have formed over millions of years through the slow deposition of mineral-rich water. Visitors to Crystal Ball Cave can marvel at the dazzling array of colors and shapes found within its chambers, from delicate draperies and curtains to massive columns and flowstones.

In addition to its crystal formations, Crystal Ball Cave is also home to a variety of unique geological features, including underground streams, pools, and chambers. Exploring the cave's labyrinthine passages offers visitors an opportunity to witness the forces of nature at work, as water and minerals interact to create stunning natural sculptures and formations.

Access to Crystal Ball Cave is limited and requires a permit from the Bureau of Land Management, as well as specialized equipment and experience in caving and spelunking. However, for those willing to undertake the journey, the cave offers a truly unforgettable experience that's sure to leave a lasting impression.

Whether you're a seasoned caver or a curious adventurer, Crystal Ball Cave offers a rare opportunity to explore the hidden wonders of Utah's underground world and discover the beauty and mystery that lie beneath the surface.

23. Fish Springs National Wildlife Refuge

Fish Springs National Wildlife Refuge, located in the remote desert of western Utah, is a haven for wildlife and bird enthusiasts seeking to explore the beauty and diversity of Utah's desert ecosystems. This pristine refuge encompasses over 17,000 acres of wetlands, springs, and marshes, providing vital habitat for a wide variety of migratory birds, waterfowl, and other wildlife species.

The centerpiece of Fish Springs National Wildlife Refuge is its namesake Fish Springs, a natural oasis fed by a series of artesian springs that bubble up from underground aquifers. These springs provide a constant source of fresh water, creating lush wetlands and marshes that support a rich diversity of plant and animal life.

Visitors to Fish Springs National Wildlife Refuge can explore a variety of habitats and ecosystems, including salt flats, alkali meadows, and desert scrubland, as well as pristine spring-fed streams and ponds. The refuge is home to a wide variety of wildlife species, including migratory birds such as waterfowl, shorebirds, and songbirds, as well as resident species such as mule deer, pronghorn antelope, and coyotes.

In addition to its wildlife viewing opportunities, Fish Springs National Wildlife Refuge offers a variety of recreational activities for visitors to enjoy. Hiking trails wind through the refuge's diverse landscapes, providing opportunities for birdwatching, photography, and nature observation, while wildlife blinds and observation platforms offer ideal vantage points for viewing and photographing the area's abundant wildlife.

Whether you're a bird enthusiast, a nature lover, or simply seeking a peaceful retreat in the desert, Fish Springs National Wildlife Refuge offers something for everyone to enjoy amidst the stunning beauty of Utah's desert wilderness.

24. Topaz Mountain

Topaz Mountain, located in the western desert of Utah, is a treasure trove of minerals and gems, offering visitors a unique opportunity to hunt for their own precious stones amidst the rugged beauty of the desert landscape. This remote mountain is renowned for its abundance of topaz crystals, as well as other minerals such as beryl, garnet, and quartz, making it a popular destination for rockhounds and gem enthusiasts from around the world.

The most prized gemstone found at Topaz Mountain is, of course, topaz, a semi-precious stone prized for its brilliant clarity and vibrant colors. Visitors to the mountain can search for topaz crystals in various colors, including clear, blue, yellow, and pink, which can be found scattered across the desert floor or embedded within the rocky outcrops and cliffs of the mountain.

In addition to topaz, Topaz Mountain is also home to a variety of other minerals and gemstones, including beryl (the mineral from which emeralds and aquamarines are formed), garnet, and quartz. Visitors can explore the mountain's rugged terrain, searching for crystals and specimens to add to their collections or turn into beautiful jewelry and keepsakes.

Access to Topaz Mountain is relatively easy, with a network of dirt roads and trails leading to various collecting areas and dig sites. However, visitors should be prepared for rugged conditions, extreme temperatures, and limited amenities, as the mountain is located in a remote and undeveloped area of the desert.

Whether you're a seasoned rockhound or a novice gem enthusiast, Topaz Mountain offers a unique and rewarding experience that's sure to delight and inspire visitors of all ages.

25. Dugway Geode Beds

The Dugway Geode Beds, located in the remote desert of western Utah, are a hidden treasure waiting to be discovered by rockhounds and geology enthusiasts. These ancient volcanic deposits are home to a variety of crystals and geodes, including quartz, calcite, and amethyst, making them a popular destination for rockhounding and gem collecting.

The geode beds are situated in a rugged and desolate landscape, with expansive vistas of desert terrain stretching as far as the eye can see. Visitors to the area can explore the desert floor, searching for geodes and crystals hidden among the rocks and sand, or hike the surrounding hillsides to take in the breathtaking views and explore the area's unique geological formations.

Geodes are spherical or oblong rock formations that contain a hollow cavity lined with crystals. The crystals form over millions of years as mineral-rich water seeps into the cavity and deposits minerals such as quartz, calcite, and amethyst. Geodes can vary in size from small, fist-sized specimens to large, football-sized formations, and are prized by collectors for their beauty and rarity.

Access to the Dugway Geode Beds is relatively easy, with a network of dirt roads and trails leading to various collecting areas and dig sites. However, visitors should be prepared for rugged conditions, extreme temperatures, and limited amenities, as the geode beds are located in a remote and undeveloped area of the desert.

Whether you're a seasoned rockhound or a novice geology enthusiast, the Dugway Geode Beds offer a unique and rewarding experience that's sure to leave a lasting impression. So grab your hammer and chisel, and get ready to unearth some hidden treasures in the Utah desert!

Colorado Plateau

1. Skyline Drive

Skyline Drive is one of Utah's most scenic and remote byways, stretching approximately 80 miles along the Wasatch Plateau. This dirt road runs primarily along the ridgeline, offering travelers breathtaking panoramic views of alpine meadows, dense forests, and distant desert landscapes. Reaching altitudes of over 10,000 feet, Skyline Drive provides a unique experience for outdoor enthusiasts looking to escape the hustle and bustle of modern life.

The drive begins near the town of Fairview and runs south, ending near I-70, traversing some of the state's most rugged and untouched wilderness. It's a perfect destination for those who love off-roading, as the road is unpaved and best suited for high-clearance vehicles. ATV and UTV riders flock to Skyline Drive during the summer months, and it's part of the extensive Arapeen OHV Trail system. However, it is equally popular with hikers, mountain bikers, and campers looking to explore the backcountry and enjoy the tranquility of nature.

One of the highlights of Skyline Drive is the incredible variety of wildlife that can be spotted along the way, including elk, deer, and various bird species. The plateau is also known for its fishing opportunities, with several reservoirs and alpine lakes nearby, such as Fairview Lakes and Huntington Reservoir.

The best time to visit is from late spring to early fall, as the road is often closed in the winter due to heavy snowfall. During the warmer months, the cool temperatures and crisp mountain air make it an ideal escape from the heat of the valleys below.

Whether you're an avid adventurer or someone looking for a peaceful retreat in nature, Skyline Drive offers unparalleled beauty and solitude, making it one of Utah's hidden gems.

2. Cleveland-Lloyd Dinosaur Quarry

The Cleveland-Lloyd Dinosaur Quarry, nestled in the heart of Utah's scenic desert landscape, is a remarkable paleontological site that has intrigued scientists and visitors alike for over a century. This extraordinary quarry is located within the Jurassic National Monument and is renowned for the density and diversity of Jurassic-era dinosaur fossils it has yielded, making it one of the most prolific dinosaur fossil sites in the world. The significance of the Cleveland-Lloyd Dinosaur Quarry extends beyond the sheer volume of bones; it provides invaluable insights into the lives and environment of the dinosaurs that roamed this area approximately 150 million years ago.

What sets the Cleveland-Lloyd Dinosaur Quarry apart is not just the quantity of the fossils found but the mystery surrounding the high concentration of carnivorous dinosaur remains. Predominantly, the quarry is famous for its extensive collection of Allosaurus fragments, a fact that puzzles scientists because it suggests an unusually high population of predators in one area. This anomaly has led to various hypotheses regarding the behavior and ecology of these ancient creatures, including theories about drought-driven mass mortality or a predatory trap that might have lured dinosaurs to their demise.

Visitors to the Cleveland-Lloyd Dinosaur Quarry can explore the Dinosaur Quarry Building, where many of the unearthed bones are displayed in situ, offering a rare glimpse into the painstaking process of paleontological excavation and research. The site also features interpretive trails and a visitor center, which provides educational exhibits on the dinosaurs discovered at the quarry, the history of the excavations, and the scientific significance of the findings.

The quarry not only serves as a critical site for scientific research but also as an educational and recreational resource, drawing enthusiasts from around the globe. It offers a unique window into the Jurassic period, enabling visitors to step back in time and marvel at the ancient world of dinosaurs. The Cleveland-Lloyd Dinosaur Quarry is a testament to the enduring fascination with these magnificent creatures and the earth's geological past, making it a must-visit for anyone interested in paleontology, natural history, or the sheer wonder of dinosaurs.

3. Swasey's Beach

Swasey's Beach, a hidden gem located near the town of Green River in Utah, offers a unique blend of natural beauty and recreational fun that stands out even in a state known for its stunning landscapes. Unlike the rugged, arid terrains commonly associated with Utah, Swasey's Beach presents a surprising contrast with its soft, sandy shores and the gentle flow of the Green River. This picturesque spot is a haven for locals and travelers seeking a peaceful retreat or a day filled with outdoor activities in a relatively untouched setting.

Nestled along a bend of the Green River, Swasey's Beach is accessible via a short drive from Green River, Utah, making it an easy getaway for those looking to escape the hustle and bustle of city life. The beach's fine sand and the river's calm waters create an inviting environment for a variety of activities, including swimming, picnicking, and sunbathing. The area is also popular among kayakers and paddleboarders, who take advantage of the serene river flow for leisurely excursions downstream.

One of the defining features of Swasey's Beach is its surrounding landscape. The beach is framed by towering cliffs and rock formations, characteristic of Utah's dramatic geology, providing a breathtaking backdrop for visitors. This setting not only enhances the beach's scenic value but also offers opportunities for photography and wildlife observation, with the local fauna frequently making appearances along the riverbanks.

Swasey's Beach is more than just a picturesque location; it's a community gathering spot where families and friends can come together to enjoy nature's tranquility. Despite its growing popularity, the beach maintains a sense of seclusion and intimacy, offering a slice of paradise where visitors can relax, play, and soak in the stunning natural surroundings.

The accessibility of Swasey's Beach, combined with its scenic beauty and the array of recreational activities it supports, makes it a beloved destination for those who discover it. It embodies the spirit of Utah's diverse landscapes, showcasing the state's ability to surprise and enchant even the most seasoned travelers. Whether you're looking for a quiet spot to unwind or a picturesque setting for your next adventure, Swasey's Beach promises a memorable experience amidst the natural splendor of the American West.

4. Arches National Park

Arches National Park is a marvel of natural architecture and a testament to the raw sculpting powers of water, ice, and temperature fluctuations over millions of years. Spanning approximately 76,679 acres, this national park is renowned for its captivating landscape of over 2,000 natural stone arches, towering spires, giant pinnacles, and balanced rocks, making it a magnet for nature lovers, photographers, and adventurers from around the globe.

The park's most iconic landmark, Delicate Arch, stands as a solitary sentinel against the backdrop of the La Sal Mountains, offering one of the most recognized natural scenes in the Western United States. The sheer scale and beauty of Delicate Arch, alongside other notable formations like Landscape Arch and Double Arch, encapsulate the essence of the park's allure. These geological wonders are not only visually stunning but also serve as a vivid reminder of the earth's dynamic history and the ongoing processes of erosion and deposition.

Arches National Park's landscape is a vivid palette of reds, oranges, and browns, changing hues with the rising and setting sun, offering an ever-evolving spectacle that continues to enchant visitors. The park's network of hiking trails and viewpoints are meticulously designed to offer access to its many natural wonders, catering to all levels of outdoor enthusiasts. From the easy, family-friendly paths leading to Landscape Arch to the more challenging trek up to Delicate Arch, there is something for everyone.

Beyond its geological treasures, Arches National Park is a haven for desert flora and fauna, hosting a variety of plants and animals adapted to the extreme environment. The park's high desert ecosystem is home to many species of birds, mammals, and plants, each playing a role in the delicate balance of this unique habitat.

Arches National Park is not just a destination; it's an experience. It invites visitors to explore its vast, surreal landscape, offering a profound connection with nature's artistry and the ancient forces that shaped our world. Whether you're capturing the perfect sunset through an archway or standing in awe beneath a towering spire, Arches provides a sense of wonder and exploration that stays with you long after you leave.

5. The San Rafael Swell

The San Rafael Swell, a vast, wild, and untamed geological feature in central Utah, is a testament to the natural forces that have shaped the Earth over millions of years. This massive uplift of sandstone, shale, and limestone, approximately 75 miles by 40 miles in size, has been sculpted by wind, water, and time into a landscape of deep canyons, towering buttes, mesas, and intriguing rock formations. Its remote and rugged terrain offers an adventure playground for hikers, rock climbers, mountain bikers, and explorers seeking solitude and a deep connection with nature.

The Swell's heart is a showcase of Utah's dramatic desert beauty, featuring a variety of landscapes from the jagged spires of the Little Grand Canyon to the intricate patterns of the San Rafael Reef. This area, largely overseen by the Bureau of Land Management, remains relatively undeveloped, preserving its wild character and enabling an authentic wilderness experience. The Swell's geological diversity is not just a feast for the eyes; it's a rich archive of Earth's history, with layers of rock revealing the passage of time, from ancient oceans to desert dunes.

Visitors to the San Rafael Swell can delve into this history by exploring the numerous slot canyons, such as Little Wild Horse Canyon, which offer a relatively accessible yet exhilarating adventure through narrow passages carved by flash floods. For those interested in human history, the region is dotted with petroglyphs and pictographs left by the Native American cultures that once inhabited these lands.

The San Rafael Swell is also a haven for stargazers. Its remote location, far from light pollution, offers some of the darkest night skies in the United States, making it an ideal spot for astronomy enthusiasts and anyone wishing to marvel at the Milky Way in all its glory.

Despite its beauty and the myriad opportunities for adventure it offers, the San Rafael Swell remains one of Utah's best-kept secrets. Its vastness and the sense of isolation it provides make it a perfect escape for those looking to explore the beauty of the American Southwest's desert landscapes away from the crowds. The Swell invites its visitors to embrace the wild, to wander its canyons and mesas, and to find peace in its ancient, rugged embrace.

6. Goblin Valley State Park

Goblin Valley State Park, nestled in the heart of Utah's desert landscape, offers a surreal and captivating experience unlike any other. This unique state park is famed for its thousands of mushroom-shaped rock formations, known as hoodoos, which dot the landscape, giving the appearance of a gathering of goblins. These whimsical formations, created over millions of years by the forces of erosion, have transformed the valley into a fantastical alien world that fascinates visitors of all ages.

Spanning approximately 3,654 acres, Goblin Valley State Park is situated between the towns of Green River and Hanksville in southern Utah. The park's otherworldly terrain has not only attracted tourists but has also served as the backdrop for films and inspired the imagination of countless photographers and artists. The valley's landscape is composed of soft sandstone, which has eroded over time into the whimsical shapes that give the park its name. The formations vary in size, from a few feet to several meters tall, creating a maze of alleys and hidden spaces waiting to be explored.

Visitors to Goblin Valley State Park can wander freely among the hoodoos, making it an exceptional place for imaginative play and exploration. Unlike many protected areas, the park encourages interaction with the natural features, allowing for up-close experiences with the formations. Hiking trails and overlooks provide stunning views of the valley and beyond, offering perspectives on the scale and beauty of the park's geological wonders.

In addition to exploring the valley itself, the park offers opportunities for camping, picnicking, and stargazing. The remote location, far from the light pollution of large cities, makes Goblin Valley a prime spot for night sky observation, with clear views of stars, planets, and the Milky Way.

Goblin Valley State Park represents a unique blend of natural history, adventure, and whimsy. It invites visitors to step into a landscape that seems to belong to another planet, where imagination runs wild, and the ancient earth speaks through its extraordinary formations. For those seeking an escape into a world of natural wonder and geological curiosity, Goblin Valley offers an unforgettable journey into the heart of Utah's desert magic.

7. Bluejohn Canyon

Bluejohn Canyon is a remote, strikingly beautiful slot canyon located in the rugged wilderness of southeastern Utah. Renowned for its narrow passages, breathtaking rock formations, and the challenge it presents to adventurers, it has become a mecca for canyoneers and hikers seeking solitude and an unparalleled natural experience. The canyon is named after a miner and outlaw, John Griffith, known as "Blue John" for the blue-colored shirts he wore. It gained international fame through the harrowing survival story of Aron Ralston, who in 2003 was forced to amputate his own arm after becoming trapped by a fallen boulder, a story that was later adapted into the movie "127 Hours."

Bluejohn Canyon is part of the Robbers Roost area, a wild and remote region that once served as a hideout for outlaws in the late 19th and early 20th centuries. The canyon itself is divided into several sections, including the Main Fork, the West Fork, and the East Fork, each offering different levels of difficulty and scenic beauty. Its narrow slot canyons, carved by the force of water over millennia, feature a range of hues from deep red to orange and purple, reflecting the changing light of the day.

Exploring Bluejohn Canyon requires preparation and respect for the natural environment. The terrain is challenging, with sections requiring rappelling, rock scrambling, and navigation through tight spaces. It is essential for visitors to be well-equipped, have technical canyoneering skills, and carry adequate water and supplies due to the arid conditions and lack of cell service.

Despite its challenges, or perhaps because of them, Bluejohn Canyon offers an unforgettable adventure for those who traverse its depths. It embodies the raw beauty and spirit of the American Southwest's vast wilderness areas. For the intrepid explorer, it presents an opportunity to test one's limits, experience profound solitude, and connect with a landscape that has remained largely untouched by human hands. In the silence of its narrow passages, one can truly feel the immense scale of geological time and the power of nature's elements at work.

8. Dead Horse Point State Park

Dead Horse Point State Park, perched atop a high plateau at an elevation of about 5,900 feet, offers one of the most breathtaking panoramas in the American West. Situated in southeastern Utah, near the town of Moab, the park is renowned for its dramatic vistas of the Colorado River and Canyonlands National Park. The park's name originates from a legend about cowboys who used the point as a natural corral for wild mustangs in the 19th century, leaving behind a group of horses that perished from exposure. Today, Dead Horse Point State Park serves as a poignant reminder of the wild and rugged history of the West, while providing visitors with unparalleled opportunities for photography, hiking, and immersing in nature's majesty.

Spanning 5,362 acres, the park's highlight is the dramatic overlook at Dead Horse Point, offering a sweeping view of the Colorado River winding 2,000 feet below. This iconic viewpoint provides a striking contrast between the deep canyons carved by the river and the vast, arid desert landscape that surrounds it. The scene is especially mesmerizing at sunrise and sunset when the play of light transforms the canyon walls into hues of orange, red, and gold.

Dead Horse Point State Park features several miles of hiking trails that wind through the desert landscape, offering access to additional scenic overlooks and opportunities to observe the local flora and fauna. The park is also a popular destination for mountain bikers, with the Intrepid Trail System providing routes for various skill levels, showcasing the area's stunning natural beauty.

For those interested in astronomy, the park's remote location and minimal light pollution make it an excellent site for stargazing. The night sky reveals a dazzling array of stars, planets, and the Milky Way, offering a profound experience of the universe's vastness.

Dead Horse Point State Park encapsulates the beauty, history, and solitude of the desert Southwest. It invites visitors to stand at the edge of vast canyons, ponder the forces of nature that sculpted this incredible landscape, and connect with the wild spirit that defines this corner of Utah. Whether seeking adventure, tranquility, or simply a place to marvel at the wonders of the natural world, Dead Horse Point provides an unforgettable backdrop.

9. The Maze

The Maze, located in the remote western section of Canyonlands National Park in Utah, is one of the most challenging and isolated areas in the United States for backcountry exploration. Renowned for its intricate and confusing network of canyons, the Maze offers an unparalleled adventure for those seeking solitude, silence, and a profound connection with untouched wilderness. This area is aptly named; its labyrinthine canyons, formed by the erosive forces of water over millions of years, create a complex puzzle of sandstone walls that are both awe-inspiring and daunting.

The Maze is not for the faint-hearted or inexperienced. Navigating its convoluted routes requires advanced backcountry skills, including route-finding, rock climbing, and the ability to be self-sufficient in a landscape that offers no amenities and is accessible only by high-clearance four-wheel-drive vehicles. Water sources are scarce, and the risks of getting lost or encountering difficulties are real and should be taken seriously. Despite these challenges, or perhaps because of them, the Maze attracts adventurers drawn to its raw beauty and the thrill of exploring one of the last true wilderness areas left in North America.

The isolation of the Maze contributes to its pristine condition and the sense of deep tranquility it offers. Visitors are likely to experience a level of solitude rarely found in today's world. The geological wonders of the Maze, from its towering vertical walls to its deep, winding canyons, are a vivid testament to the power of natural forces. The area is also rich in cultural history, with ancient Native American rock art and ruins dotting the landscape, adding a layer of mystery to the exploration.

Adventures in the Maze require careful planning, respect for the desert environment, and an awareness of the physical and navigational challenges. However, for those who venture into its depths, the Maze offers an unforgettable experience—a journey into a wild and untamed landscape that challenges the spirit and inspires awe at the natural world's beauty and complexity.

10. Canyonlands National Park

Canyonlands National Park, located in southeastern Utah, encompasses over 337,000 acres of dramatic desert landscape carved by the Colorado River and its tributaries. The park is divided into four distinct districts: Island in the Sky, The Needles, The Maze, and the rivers themselves, each offering a unique perspective on the vast wilderness of rock, canyons, mesas, and buttes that define the Colorado Plateau.

Island in the Sky, the most accessible district, sits atop a massive 1,500-foot mesa, providing panoramic views that stretch over 100 miles on clear days. This mesa is bordered by sheer sandstone cliffs, offering visitors a bird's eye view of the park's complex canyon systems. The district features a scenic drive along the mesa's rim and several short hikes leading to spectacular overlooks, including Mesa Arch, a popular spot for sunrise photography.

The Needles district, named for its colorful spires of Cedar Mesa Sandstone, presents a more rugged and remote experience. Hiking trails in this area lead through dramatic landscapes of rock spires, arches, and ancient Puebloan ruins. The Needles offers a deeper exploration of the park's backcountry, requiring more time and effort to traverse its diverse terrain.

The Maze, as its name suggests, is the most challenging and remote part of Canyonlands, a true wilderness area known for its labyrinthine canyons. This district is a haven for experienced adventurers seeking solitude and a primitive desert experience. Access to The Maze typically requires high-clearance, four-wheel-drive vehicles and a high level of self-sufficiency.

The rivers—the Colorado and Green—carve through the heart of Canyonlands, creating a diverse and dynamic environment. River activities, such as whitewater rafting and kayaking, offer an exhilarating way to experience the park's stunning scenery from a different vantage point.

Canyonlands National Park is a place of immense geological interest, a testament to the power of water and time to sculpt the earth. Its vast landscapes inspire awe and provide endless opportunities for adventure, exploration, and contemplation.

11. The Needles

The Needles district, one of Canyonlands National Park's four distinct sections, offers a breathtaking landscape that captivates the imagination with its towering rock spires, deep canyons, and vast, open spaces. Located in the southeastern part of the park, The Needles is named for the colorful sandstone spires that dominate the area, resembling the needles of giant pines reaching towards the sky. This area presents a stark contrast to the mesa-top views of Island in the Sky, offering instead a close-up experience of the park's intricate geology and vast, undisturbed wilderness.

Characterized by a more rugged and remote environment, The Needles attracts those seeking adventure and solitude. The district's extensive network of trails invites hikers and backpackers to explore its rich tapestry of natural and cultural wonders. Among these, the Chesler Park Loop and the Joint Trail stand out, leading adventurers through narrow slot canyons, past remarkable rock formations, and into the heart of the Needles' iconic spires. These trails offer a unique blend of physical challenge and scenic reward, showcasing the area's dramatic beauty and geological complexity.

The Needles is not just a paradise for hikers; it also holds significant historical and cultural value. The area is dotted with remnants of ancient Puebloan civilization, including petroglyphs and granaries, which offer a glimpse into the lives of the Native Americans who once inhabited this land. These cultural sites add a layer of depth to the exploration of The Needles, reminding visitors of the human history that is intertwined with the natural landscape.

Access to The Needles requires a drive from Moab, Utah, and its remoteness contributes to its unspoiled beauty. Visitors to this part of Canyonlands National Park will find fewer amenities and less development than in more accessible areas, emphasizing the importance of preparation and self-sufficiency. However, the rewards of venturing into The Needles are immense, offering an immersive experience in one of the American Southwest's most spectacular natural settings. For those willing to explore its depths, The Needles promises adventure, solitude, and a profound connection with the ancient landscape.

12. Bear Ears National Monument

Bears Ears National Monument, a sprawling expanse of over 1.3 million acres located in southeastern Utah, represents a landscape of profound natural beauty and deep cultural significance. Named for the distinctive twin buttes that rise majestically above the horizon, resembling the ears of a bear, this monument encompasses a diverse ecosystem ranging from high desert to dense forest, rich in a variety of plant and animal life. The area's vast, undulating terrains of canyons, mesas, and rock formations are a testament to the enduring forces of nature that have shaped this land over millions of years.

Bears Ears is not only celebrated for its geological wonders but also revered for its historical and cultural importance. The land is considered sacred by many Native American tribes, including the Navajo, Hopi, Ute, Ute Mountain Ute, and Zuni peoples, who have inhabited this region for thousands of years. The monument is rich in ancient artifacts, petroglyphs, and ceremonial sites, offering a window into the lives of the Indigenous peoples who have called this place home. The designation of Bears Ears as a national monument in 2016 was a historic victory for these tribes, who united to advocate for the protection of their ancestral lands.

Visitors to Bears Ears National Monument can explore a vast network of trails that offer access to some of the monument's most stunning landscapes and archaeological sites. From the Valley of the Gods, with its towering sandstone formations, to the intricate petroglyph panels at Newspaper Rock, the monument offers endless opportunities for exploration and discovery. Hiking, climbing, and backpacking are popular activities, allowing adventurers to immerse themselves in the natural beauty and solitude of the area.

The creation of Bears Ears National Monument marked a significant step in recognizing the importance of preserving America's natural landscapes and cultural heritage. It serves as a reminder of the deep connections between land and people, inviting visitors to explore and respect the sacredness of this extraordinary place. As a symbol of collaboration between the U.S. government and Native American tribes, Bears Ears stands as a testament to the value of protecting our nation's most precious resources for future generations.

13. Edge of the Cedars State Park Museum

Nestled in the heart of Utah's majestic landscape, Edge of the Cedars State Park Museum stands as a testament to the rich cultural heritage of the region. Located near Blanding, this museum offers visitors a fascinating journey through time, exploring the history and archaeology of the ancestral Puebloan people who once thrived in the area.

The museum's name derives from its proximity to a stand of ancient cedar trees that line the nearby cliff edges. These trees, along with the rugged terrain and sweeping vistas, provide a stunning backdrop to the museum's exhibits.

Upon entering the museum, visitors are greeted by a comprehensive collection of artifacts spanning thousands of years of human history in the region. From intricately crafted pottery to finely wrought tools and ceremonial objects, each item tells a story of the people who inhabited this land long ago.

One of the highlights of the museum is its extensive collection of Ancestral Puebloan pottery, considered some of the finest examples of prehistoric ceramics in the Southwest. These beautifully decorated vessels offer insights into the artistic and cultural achievements of the ancient inhabitants.

In addition to its indoor exhibits, Edge of the Cedars State Park Museum also features an outdoor archaeological site where visitors can explore the remains of an ancient Puebloan village. Walking among the partially reconstructed structures, visitors can envision what life was like for the people who called this place home centuries ago.

For those interested in learning more about the archaeology of the region, the museum offers educational programs, guided tours, and special events throughout the year. Whether you're a history enthusiast, an archaeology buff, or simply someone who appreciates the natural beauty of the Southwest, Edge of the Cedars State Park Museum is a must-visit destination.

14. Natural Bridges National Monument

Tucked away in the rugged landscape of southern Utah, Natural Bridges National Monument is a place of breathtaking natural beauty and cultural significance. This hidden gem of the Southwest is home to three majestic natural bridges carved by the forces of wind and water over millions of years.

The largest of these bridges, named Sipapu by the Native American tribes of the region, spans an impressive 268 feet across and stands 220 feet high. As the symbol of the monument, Sipapu serves as a reminder of the powerful forces of erosion that have shaped this landscape over time.

In addition to Sipapu, visitors to the monument can also marvel at the beauty of Kachina and Owachomo bridges, each with its own unique characteristics and charm. Whether seen from overlooks along the scenic drive or explored up close on hiking trails, these natural wonders never fail to inspire awe and wonder.

Beyond its natural beauty, Natural Bridges National Monument is also rich in cultural history. For centuries, the area has been home to various Native American tribes, who have left their mark in the form of petroglyphs, pictographs, and ancient ruins scattered throughout the landscape.

Visitors to the monument can learn about the cultural significance of these sites through interpretive exhibits and ranger-led programs. From the mysterious rock art of the Ancestral Puebloans to the stories of the modern-day descendants of the region's indigenous peoples, there is much to discover about the human history of Natural Bridges National Monument.

Whether you're a nature lover, a history buff, or simply someone in search of tranquility and solitude, Natural Bridges National Monument offers a truly unforgettable experience. With its stunning natural scenery, rich cultural heritage, and opportunities for exploration and discovery, this hidden gem of the Southwest is not to be missed.

15. House on Fire Ruins

Nestled deep within the rugged canyons of Utah's Cedar Mesa, the House on Fire Ruins is a hidden archaeological gem that captivates visitors with its remarkable beauty and historical significance. Named for the striking resemblance of its sandstone alcove to flames leaping from a hearth, this ancient ruin offers a glimpse into the lives of the ancestral Puebloan people who once inhabited this area.

The ruins consist of several well-preserved structures built into the alcove's natural recesses, including rooms, kivas, and storage areas. Despite being abandoned for centuries, the vibrant hues of the sandstone walls and the intricate masonry of the structures still evoke a sense of the bustling community that once thrived here.

One of the most intriguing features of the House on Fire Ruins is the elaborate rock art that adorns the alcove walls. These ancient pictographs, created by the ancestral Puebloans using pigments made from natural minerals, depict a variety of symbols and motifs that offer clues to their beliefs, customs, and way of life.

Visitors to the ruins can access the site via a moderate hike along a scenic canyon trail. Along the way, hikers are treated to breathtaking views of the surrounding landscape, including towering sandstone cliffs, winding slot canyons, and lush desert vegetation.

While the House on Fire Ruins may be off the beaten path, its remote location only adds to its allure. Far from the crowds and commercialization of more popular tourist destinations, this hidden archaeological treasure offers visitors a rare opportunity to connect with the ancient past in a tranquil and unspoiled setting.

Whether you're an avid hiker, a history enthusiast, or simply someone who appreciates the beauty of the natural world, a visit to the House on Fire Ruins is sure to be a memorable experience. With its stunning scenery, rich cultural heritage, and sense of mystery and wonder, this hidden gem of the Southwest is truly a must-see destination.

16. Hovenweep National Monument

Nestled on the rugged borderlands of southeastern Utah and southwestern Colorado, Hovenweep National Monument is a testament to the ingenuity and resilience of the ancient Puebloan people. This remote and lesser-known destination offers visitors a chance to step back in time and explore a landscape dotted with ancient stone structures, mysterious ruins, and breathtaking natural beauty.

The centerpiece of Hovenweep National Monument is its collection of six prehistoric villages, each featuring a unique array of multi-story towers, kivas, and other architectural marvels. These structures, built between the 12th and 13th centuries, stand as silent sentinels to the thriving communities that once inhabited this region.

Among the most impressive sites within the monument is the Square Tower Group, where visitors can marvel at the intricately constructed towers that give the site its name. Perched on the edge of a sandstone canyon, these ancient structures offer stunning panoramic views of the surrounding landscape.

In addition to its archaeological wonders, Hovenweep National Monument is also home to a diverse array of natural attractions. From towering rock formations and sweeping desert vistas to lush riparian corridors and colorful wildflower blooms, the monument's landscape is a feast for the senses.

Visitors to Hovenweep National Monument can explore the area's rich history and natural beauty through a variety of hiking trails, interpretive exhibits, and ranger-led programs. Whether wandering among the ancient ruins, birdwatching along the banks of a winding stream, or simply soaking in the quiet solitude of the desert, there is much to discover and enjoy in this hidden gem of the American Southwest.

17. Valley of the Gods

Tucked away in the southeastern corner of Utah, not far from the better-known Monument Valley, lies a hidden treasure known as the Valley of the Gods. This remote and stunning landscape is characterized by towering sandstone buttes, sculpted rock formations, and sweeping desert vistas that rival those found anywhere in the American West.

Despite its proximity to Monument Valley, the Valley of the Gods remains relatively undiscovered by tourists, making it an ideal destination for those seeking solitude and tranquility amid nature's grandeur. Visitors to the valley can explore its scenic wonders via a 17-mile dirt road that winds its way through the heart of the landscape, offering numerous opportunities for hiking, photography, and sightseeing along the way.

One of the highlights of the Valley of the Gods is its unique rock formations, which have been sculpted by the forces of wind and water over millions of years. From towering spires and sheer cliffs to labyrinthine canyons and hidden alcoves, the landscape is a playground for outdoor enthusiasts and adventure seekers alike.

In addition to its natural beauty, the Valley of the Gods is also steeped in history and legend. For centuries, the area has been sacred to the indigenous Navajo people, who consider it a place of spiritual significance and reverence. Visitors to the valley can learn about its cultural heritage through interpretive exhibits, guided tours, and interactions with local Navajo guides.

Whether you're a seasoned traveler or a first-time visitor to the American Southwest, the Valley of the Gods offers a truly unforgettable experience. With its stunning scenery, rich cultural history, and sense of remote wilderness, this hidden gem is sure to leave a lasting impression on all who venture into its midst.

18. Mexican Hat

Perched on the banks of the San Juan River in southeastern Utah, the small town of Mexican Hat is a charming oasis amid the rugged beauty of the American Southwest. Named for a nearby rock formation that resembles a traditional Mexican sombrero, this quaint hamlet offers visitors a chance to experience the unique blend of history, culture, and natural beauty that defines this corner of the world.

One of the main attractions in Mexican Hat is, of course, the iconic rock formation that gives the town its name. Towering over the surrounding landscape, the "Mexican Hat" is a popular spot for photography, sightseeing, and even rock climbing for the more adventurous visitors.

In addition to its namesake rock formation, Mexican Hat is also a gateway to some of the Southwest's most spectacular natural wonders. Nearby attractions include the Valley of the Gods, Goosenecks State Park, and Monument Valley, each offering its own unique blend of stunning scenery and outdoor adventure opportunities.

Despite its small size, Mexican Hat boasts a rich history and cultural heritage that is evident in its architecture, cuisine, and way of life. Visitors to the town can explore its historic buildings, browse local art galleries and shops, and sample authentic Southwestern cuisine at one of its charming cafes or restaurants.

Whether you're seeking adventure in the great outdoors or simply looking to soak in the beauty and tranquility of the desert landscape, Mexican Hat offers something for everyone. With its stunning scenery, rich history, and warm hospitality, this hidden gem of the American Southwest is sure to leave a lasting impression on all who visit.

19. Goosenecks State Park

Nestled along the meandering course of the San Juan River in southeastern Utah, Goosenecks State Park offers visitors a mesmerizing vista of one of nature's most impressive geological formations. The park's main attraction is a series of deep, narrow canyons carved over millions of years by the winding river, creating a breathtaking display of zigzagging twists and turns that resemble the neck of a goose.

From the park's overlooks, visitors can gaze down into the depths of the canyon, where the river has sculpted intricate layers of sandstone and shale, revealing millions of years of geological history. The sheer scale of the canyons, combined with the vibrant colors of the rock formations and the serpentine path of the river below, creates a scene of unparalleled beauty and tranquility.

In addition to its stunning natural scenery, Goosenecks State Park also offers opportunities for hiking, picnicking, and stargazing. The park's remote location and lack of light pollution make it an ideal spot for observing the night sky, with millions of stars twinkling overhead and the Milky Way stretching across the horizon in a dazzling display.

For those interested in learning more about the geology and natural history of the area, the park offers interpretive exhibits and ranger-led programs that provide insights into the forces that shaped this unique landscape. Whether you're a seasoned outdoor enthusiast or simply someone in search of quiet solitude amid nature's grandeur, Goosenecks State Park offers a truly unforgettable experience.

20. Moki Dugway

Located in southeastern Utah's rugged Cedar Mesa region, the Moki Dugway is a breathtakingly scenic stretch of road that winds its way up the side of Cedar Mesa via a series of hairpin turns and switchbacks. Carved into the face of the mesa by miners in the 1950s, the road offers stunning panoramic views of the surrounding landscape, including the nearby Valley of the Gods, Monument Valley, and the distant peaks of the La Sal Mountains.

Named for the Moki (a term used by early settlers to refer to the indigenous Puebloan people) and the Navajo term for a trail or path, the Moki Dugway is both a marvel of engineering and a testament to the human spirit's ability to conquer even the most challenging terrain. As you ascend the steep grades and navigate the tight curves of the road, you'll be treated to sweeping vistas of towering rock formations, deep canyons, and vast desert expanses stretching as far as the eye can see.

For adventurous travelers, the Moki Dugway is not only a scenic drive but also a gateway to some of the Southwest's most spectacular natural wonders. Nearby attractions include Goosenecks State Park, Valley of the Gods, and Monument Valley, each offering its own unique blend of stunning scenery and outdoor adventure opportunities.

Whether you're a thrill-seeking road tripper or simply someone in search of awe-inspiring views and rugged beauty, the Moki Dugway promises an unforgettable journey through some of the most breathtaking landscapes in the American West.

21. Monument Valley

Iconic, majestic, and utterly mesmerizing, Monument Valley stands as a timeless symbol of the American Southwest's rugged beauty and ancient history. Located on the Arizona-Utah border within the Navajo Nation Reservation, this iconic landscape is characterized by its towering sandstone buttes, mesas, and spires that rise dramatically from the desert floor, creating a scene that is both otherworldly and awe-inspiring.

Made famous by countless Western films and television shows, Monument Valley has captured the imaginations of travelers and adventurers from around the world for generations. From the imposing silhouette of the Mittens and Merrick Butte to the iconic formations of Elephant Butte and Camel Butte, the valley's landmarks are as iconic as they are breathtaking.

In addition to its stunning natural scenery, Monument Valley is also rich in cultural history and heritage. For centuries, the area has been sacred to the Navajo people, who consider it a place of spiritual significance and reverence. Visitors to the valley can learn about its cultural heritage through interpretive exhibits, guided tours, and interactions with local Navajo guides.

One of the best ways to experience Monument Valley is by taking a scenic drive along the Valley Drive, a 17-mile loop road that winds its way through the heart of the landscape, offering numerous opportunities for photography, sightseeing, and exploration along the way. For those seeking a more immersive experience, guided tours and hiking excursions are also available, allowing visitors to delve deeper into the valley's secrets and mysteries.

Whether you're a seasoned traveler or a first-time visitor to the American Southwest, Monument Valley offers a truly unforgettable experience. With its stunning scenery, rich cultural heritage, and sense of timeless beauty, this iconic landscape is sure to leave a lasting impression on all who venture into its midst.

22. Glen Canyon National Recreation Area

Nestled in the heart of the American Southwest, Glen Canyon National Recreation Area is a vast and stunning landscape of towering sandstone cliffs, deep canyons, and shimmering waterways. Encompassing over 1.25 million acres of land in southern Utah and northern Arizona, this iconic destination offers visitors a wealth of outdoor recreational opportunities amid some of the most breathtaking scenery in the country.

At the heart of Glen Canyon National Recreation Area is the mighty Colorado River, whose meandering course has carved out the majestic Glen Canyon over millions of years. The centerpiece of the recreation area is Lake Powell, a sprawling reservoir created by the construction of Glen Canyon Dam in the 1960s. Stretching over 180 miles in length and boasting over 2,000 miles of shoreline, Lake Powell is a paradise for water enthusiasts, offering opportunities for boating, fishing, swimming, and kayaking amid stunning desert landscapes.

In addition to its water-based activities, Glen Canyon National Recreation Area is also a haven for hikers, backpackers, and outdoor adventurers. With hundreds of miles of hiking trails, ranging from easy strolls to challenging backcountry routes, visitors can explore the region's rugged terrain, hidden slot canyons, and ancient rock art sites.

For those interested in learning more about the area's natural and cultural history, the recreation area is home to several visitor centers and interpretive exhibits that provide insights into the geology, ecology, and human history of the region. From the ancient Ancestral Puebloan ruins of Horseshoe Bend to the iconic sandstone arches of Rainbow Bridge, there is much to discover and explore within Glen Canyon National Recreation Area.

Whether you're a nature lover, an outdoor enthusiast, or simply someone in search of peace and tranquility amid stunning natural beauty, Glen Canyon National Recreation Area offers something for everyone. With its diverse array of recreational opportunities, breathtaking scenery, and sense of remote wilderness, this iconic destination is sure to leave a lasting impression on all who visit.

23. Rainbow Bridge National Monument

Tucked away in a remote corner of southern Utah, Rainbow Bridge National Monument is a natural wonder of breathtaking beauty and cultural significance. Carved over millions of years by the erosive forces of wind and water, Rainbow Bridge stands as one of the largest natural bridges in the world, spanning an impressive 290 feet in height and 275 feet in width.

For centuries, Rainbow Bridge has been revered by the indigenous Navajo people, who consider it a sacred and spiritual place. According to Navajo legend, the bridge was formed by the hands of the gods as a symbol of their divine power and protection. Today, the monument remains an important pilgrimage site for the Navajo and other Native American tribes, who come to pay homage to this natural wonder and connect with their cultural heritage.

Visitors to Rainbow Bridge National Monument can access the bridge via a scenic boat ride on Lake Powell or a challenging hike through rugged desert terrain. Along the way, hikers are treated to stunning views of the surrounding landscape, including towering sandstone cliffs, hidden slot canyons, and colorful desert flora.

Despite its remote location and the challenges of reaching it, Rainbow Bridge National Monument continues to attract visitors from around the world who come to marvel at its beauty and significance. Whether seen from a boat on Lake Powell or up close on foot, the bridge's graceful arch and vibrant hues never fail to inspire awe and wonder.

In addition to its natural beauty, Rainbow Bridge National Monument is also home to a diverse array of plant and animal life, including desert bighorn sheep, coyotes, and a variety of migratory birds. For those interested in learning more about the monument's natural and cultural history, interpretive exhibits and ranger-led programs are available at the nearby visitor center.

Whether you're a seasoned hiker, a nature enthusiast, or simply someone in search of inspiration and wonder, Rainbow Bridge National Monument offers a truly unforgettable experience. With its stunning scenery, rich cultural heritage, and sense of timeless beauty, this natural wonder is sure to leave a lasting impression on all who visit.

24. Lake Powell

Stretching over 180 miles across the desert landscape of southern Utah and northern Arizona, Lake Powell is a vast and stunning reservoir that offers visitors a wealth of recreational opportunities amid some of the most breathtaking scenery in the American Southwest. Created by the construction of Glen Canyon Dam in the 1960s, the lake is a paradise for water enthusiasts, offering opportunities for boating, fishing, swimming, and kayaking amid towering sandstone cliffs, hidden slot canyons, and colorful desert vistas.

With over 2,000 miles of shoreline and countless secluded coves and beaches, Lake Powell provides endless opportunities for exploration and adventure. Visitors can rent houseboats, speedboats, or kayaks and set out to discover the lake's hidden treasures, from remote slot canyons accessible only by water to picturesque sandy beaches perfect for picnicking and sunbathing.

In addition to its water-based activities, Lake Powell is also a popular destination for hiking, camping, and sightseeing. The surrounding landscape is home to a wealth of natural wonders, including the iconic sandstone formations of Rainbow Bridge, the towering cliffs of Horseshoe Bend, and the ancient Ancestral Puebloan ruins of Navajo Canyon.

For those interested in learning more about the area's natural and cultural history, Lake Powell is home to several visitor centers and interpretive exhibits that provide insights into the geology, ecology, and human history of the region. Whether you're exploring the lake's tranquil waters, hiking through the surrounding desert landscape, or simply soaking in the stunning scenery from the shore, Lake Powell offers something for everyone.

Whether you're a seasoned outdoor enthusiast or simply someone in search of relaxation and adventure amid stunning natural beauty, Lake Powell is sure to leave a lasting impression on all who visit. With its vast expanse of shimmering water, towering sandstone cliffs, and endless opportunities for exploration and discovery, this iconic destination is truly a gem of the American Southwest.

25. Buckskin Gulch

Nestled within the remote and rugged landscape of southern Utah, Buckskin Gulch is a breathtaking slot canyon that captivates visitors with its towering walls, twisted rock formations, and ethereal beauty. Widely regarded as one of the longest and deepest slot canyons in the world, Buckskin Gulch offers a truly immersive and awe-inspiring outdoor adventure for hikers and photographers alike.

Stretching for over 15 miles through the heart of the Paria Canyon-Vermilion Cliffs Wilderness Area, Buckskin Gulch is a testament to the power of water and erosion to sculpt the landscape over millions of years. The canyon's narrow passages and towering walls, carved from the Navajo Sandstone by the relentless force of flash floods and flowing water, create a surreal and otherworldly environment that seems to defy the passage of time.

For adventurous hikers, exploring Buckskin Gulch is an unforgettable experience. The canyon's winding corridors, intricate twists and turns, and hidden alcoves offer endless opportunities for discovery and exploration. From navigating through narrow slot sections barely wide enough to squeeze through to marveling at the towering rock formations and hidden waterfalls that dot the landscape, every step reveals a new wonder to behold.

In addition to its stunning natural beauty, Buckskin Gulch is also home to a rich array of flora and fauna, including desert bighorn sheep, coyotes, and a variety of bird species. For those interested in learning more about the area's natural and cultural history, interpretive exhibits and ranger-led programs are available at the nearby Paria Contact Station.

Whether you're a seasoned adventurer or simply someone in search of tranquility and solitude amid nature's grandeur, Buckskin Gulch offers a truly unforgettable experience. With its towering walls, twisting passages, and sense of remote wilderness, this iconic slot canyon is sure to leave a lasting impression on all who venture into its depths.

26. The Wave Trail

Hidden away in the remote desert landscape of southern Utah, The Wave is a geological marvel that defies description and captivates visitors with its otherworldly beauty. Formed over millions of years by the erosive forces of wind and water, this iconic sandstone formation features a series of undulating waves, swirling patterns, and vibrant colors that create a surreal and mesmerizing landscape.

Located within the Coyote Buttes North Wilderness Area, The Wave is accessible via a challenging hiking trail that winds its way through a rugged and desolate landscape of sandstone mesas, deep canyons, and sculpted rock formations. Along the way, hikers are treated to stunning views of the surrounding desert scenery, including towering cliffs, hidden arches, and colorful sandstone hoodoos.

As you approach The Wave, the landscape begins to change, with the smooth, undulating curves of the sandstone formations coming into view. With each step, the colors and patterns of the rock seem to shift and change, creating an ever-changing kaleidoscope of shapes and textures that mesmerize the senses.

For photographers, The Wave is a dream come true, offering endless opportunities for capturing stunning images of this natural wonder. From the soft light of sunrise to the warm glow of sunset, the changing colors and textures of the rock formations create a magical backdrop for capturing the beauty of the desert landscape.

Due to its remote location and fragile ecosystem, access to The Wave is limited, with only a small number of permits issued each day through a lottery system. However, for those lucky enough to secure a permit, the experience of exploring this iconic landscape is truly unforgettable.

Whether you're a seasoned hiker, a photographer, or simply someone in search of adventure and exploration, The Wave offers a once-in-a-lifetime opportunity to experience the beauty and wonder of one of nature's most remarkable creations.

27. Coral Pink Sand Dunes State Park

Nestled amidst the vibrant desert landscape of southern Utah, Coral Pink Sand Dunes State Park is a hidden gem that offers visitors a unique and unforgettable outdoor adventure. This iconic destination is home to a stunning expanse of rolling sand dunes, whose vibrant hues range from pale pink to deep coral, creating a landscape that is both surreal and mesmerizing.

Formed over thousands of years by the erosion of Navajo Sandstone deposits, the dunes of Coral Pink Sand Dunes State Park are constantly shifting and changing, sculpted by the relentless forces of wind and weather. As you explore the park, you'll be treated to breathtaking views of towering dunes, sweeping vistas, and colorful desert vegetation, creating a scene that seems to belong to another world entirely.

For outdoor enthusiasts, Coral Pink Sand Dunes State Park offers a wealth of recreational opportunities. Visitors can hike, sandboard, or ride off-highway vehicles (OHVs) on the park's designated trails, or simply relax and soak in the beauty of the desert landscape. With over 3,700 acres of pristine wilderness to explore, there's no shortage of adventures to be had in this unique and enchanting destination.

In addition to its outdoor activities, Coral Pink Sand Dunes State Park is also home to a diverse array of plant and animal life, including desert sagebrush, juniper trees, and a variety of bird species. For those interested in learning more about the area's natural history, interpretive exhibits and ranger-led programs are available at the park's visitor center.

Whether you're a nature lover, an outdoor enthusiast, or simply someone in search of tranquility and solitude amid stunning natural beauty, Coral Pink Sand Dunes State Park offers something for everyone. With its vibrant colors, sweeping vistas, and sense of remote wilderness, this hidden gem of the American Southwest is sure to leave a lasting impression on all who visit.

28. Sand Hollow State Park

Located in the heart of southern Utah's red rock country, Sand Hollow State Park is a stunning oasis of outdoor recreation and natural beauty. Boasting shimmering blue waters, towering red sandstone cliffs, and sprawling desert vistas, this iconic destination offers visitors a wealth of opportunities for adventure and relaxation amid some of the most breathtaking scenery in the American Southwest.

The centerpiece of Sand Hollow State Park is its sprawling reservoir, whose crystal-clear waters are perfect for swimming, boating, fishing, and other water-based activities. Whether you're paddling along the shoreline in a kayak, gliding across the water on a stand-up paddleboard, or zooming around on a jet ski, there's no shortage of ways to enjoy the park's sparkling waters.

In addition to its water-based activities, Sand Hollow State Park is also home to miles of scenic hiking and biking trails that wind their way through the surrounding desert landscape. From easy strolls along the shoreline to challenging treks through rugged canyons and mesas, there's a trail for every skill level and interest.

For those looking to extend their stay, Sand Hollow State Park offers a variety of camping options, including tent and RV sites, as well as cozy cabins and yurts. With its stunning sunsets, clear night skies, and sense of remote wilderness, camping at Sand Hollow is an unforgettable experience that allows visitors to truly immerse themselves in the beauty of the desert landscape.

Whether you're a thrill-seeking adventurer, a nature lover, or simply someone in search of relaxation and tranquility amid stunning natural beauty, Sand Hollow State Park offers something for everyone. With its diverse array of recreational opportunities, breathtaking scenery, and warm desert climate, this iconic destination is sure to leave a lasting impression on all who visit.

29. Zion National Park

Encompassing over 230 square miles of stunning desert landscape in southwestern Utah, Zion National Park is a world-renowned destination that captivates visitors with its towering sandstone cliffs, verdant river valleys, and cascading waterfalls. From the iconic red rock formations of the Zion Canyon to the tranquil beauty of the Virgin River Narrows, this iconic park offers a wealth of outdoor adventures and natural wonders waiting to be explored.

The crown jewel of Zion National Park is Zion Canyon, a breathtaking gorge carved over millions of years by the flowing waters of the Virgin River. Towering sandstone cliffs rise thousands of feet above the canyon floor, creating a dramatic backdrop for hiking, rock climbing, and sightseeing. Popular hikes include the iconic Angel's Landing, which offers stunning panoramic views of the canyon below, and the Narrows, where hikers can wade through the shallow waters of the Virgin River as it winds its way through towering slot canyons.

In addition to its stunning geological features, Zion National Park is also home to a diverse array of plant and animal life, including desert bighorn sheep, mule deer, and golden eagles. Visitors can learn more about the park's natural history and cultural heritage through interpretive exhibits, ranger-led programs, and guided tours.

For those looking to extend their stay, Zion National Park offers a variety of camping options, from rustic tent sites to cozy cabins and lodges. With its stunning scenery, rich biodiversity, and sense of remote wilderness, camping in Zion is an unforgettable experience that allows visitors to truly connect with nature.

Whether you're a seasoned hiker, a nature enthusiast, or simply someone in search of awe-inspiring beauty and tranquility, Zion National Park offers something for everyone. With its iconic landscapes, diverse recreational opportunities, and warm desert climate, this legendary destination is sure to leave a lasting impression on all who visit.

30. Cedar Breaks National Monument

Perched high atop the Markagunt Plateau in southwestern Utah, Cedar Breaks National Monument is a hidden gem of the American Southwest, offering visitors a stunning panorama of colorful rock formations, deep canyons, and lush alpine meadows. Often referred to as "Utah's Bryce Canyon," Cedar Breaks boasts similar geological features to its more famous neighbor but on a smaller, more intimate scale.

At the heart of Cedar Breaks National Monument is the Cedar Breaks Amphitheater, a breathtaking natural amphitheater carved from the vibrant red and orange limestone of the Claron Formation. Towering hoodoos, spires, and pinnacles rise hundreds of feet above the canyon floor, creating a surreal and otherworldly landscape that seems to belong to another time and place.

In addition to its stunning geological formations, Cedar Breaks National Monument is also home to a diverse array of plant and animal life, including wildflowers, pinyon pines, and mule deer. Visitors can explore the park's scenic overlooks, hiking trails, and interpretive exhibits, learning more about the area's natural history and cultural heritage along the way.

For those looking to extend their stay, Cedar Breaks National Monument offers a variety of camping options, including tent sites and RV hookups. With its clear night skies and minimal light pollution, camping in Cedar Breaks is an unforgettable experience that allows visitors to gaze in wonder at the Milky Way and other celestial wonders.

Whether you're a seasoned hiker, a nature enthusiast, or simply someone in search of tranquility and solitude amid stunning natural beauty, Cedar Breaks National Monument offers something for everyone. With its iconic landscapes, diverse recreational opportunities, and sense of remote wilderness, this hidden gem of the American Southwest is sure to leave a lasting impression on all who visit.

31. Bryce Canyon National Park

Nestled in the heart of southern Utah's red rock country, Bryce Canyon National Park is a geological wonderland of stunning rock formations, towering hoodoos, and breathtaking vistas. Renowned for its unique and otherworldly landscape, the park offers visitors a chance to explore a maze of colorful amphitheaters, natural bridges, and slot canyons carved from the vibrant red and orange limestone of the Claron Formation.

The centerpiece of Bryce Canyon National Park is the Bryce Amphitheater, a sprawling basin carved by the erosive forces of wind and water over millions of years. Towering hoodoos, sculpted arches, and delicate spires rise hundreds of feet above the canyon floor, creating a surreal and mesmerizing landscape that seems to defy the laws of nature.

For outdoor enthusiasts, Bryce Canyon National Park offers a wealth of recreational opportunities, including hiking, horseback riding, and cross-country skiing. The park's extensive network of trails winds its way through the scenic landscape, offering stunning views of the surrounding rock formations and wildlife encounters with mule deer, elk, and even the occasional mountain lion.

One of the most popular hikes in the park is the Navajo Loop Trail, which descends into the heart of the Bryce Amphitheater, passing by iconic landmarks such as Wall Street and Thor's Hammer. For those seeking a more challenging adventure, the Fairyland Loop Trail offers a longer and more strenuous hike with equally stunning views of the park's unique rock formations.

In addition to its natural beauty, Bryce Canyon National Park is also home to a rich array of plant and animal life, including ponderosa pines, Utah junipers, and a variety of bird species. Visitors can learn more about the park's natural and cultural history through interpretive exhibits, ranger-led programs, and guided tours.

Whether you're a seasoned hiker, a nature lover, or simply someone in search of awe-inspiring beauty and tranquility, Bryce Canyon National Park offers something for everyone.

32. Kodachrome Basin State Park

Tucked away in the remote desert landscape of southern Utah, Kodachrome Basin State Park is a hidden gem that captivates visitors with its stunning rock formations, colorful sandstone spires, and vibrant desert flora. Named for its resemblance to the vivid colors of Kodachrome film, this iconic destination offers a truly immersive outdoor adventure amid some of the most breathtaking scenery in the American Southwest.

The centerpiece of Kodachrome Basin State Park is its collection of towering sandstone chimneys, which rise hundreds of feet above the desert floor and create a surreal and otherworldly landscape. Formed over millions of years by the erosive forces of wind and water, these unique rock formations come alive with color and texture, creating a photographer's paradise and a hiker's dream.

For outdoor enthusiasts, Kodachrome Basin State Park offers a variety of recreational opportunities, including hiking, mountain biking, and horseback riding. The park's extensive network of trails winds its way through the scenic landscape, offering stunning views of the surrounding rock formations and glimpses of wildlife such as mule deer, coyotes, and desert cottontails.

One of the most popular hikes in the park is the Angel's Palace Trail, which leads visitors through a maze of towering sandstone spires and offers panoramic views of the surrounding desert landscape. For those seeking a more leisurely adventure, the Panorama Trail offers a scenic drive through the park, with numerous overlooks and picnic areas perfect for enjoying the beauty of the desert scenery.

In addition to its natural beauty, Kodachrome Basin State Park is also home to a rich array of plant and animal life, including sagebrush, prickly pear cactus, and a variety of bird species. Visitors can learn more about the park's natural and cultural history through interpretive exhibits, ranger-led programs, and guided tours.

33. Grand Staircase-Escalante National Monument

Spanning over 1.9 million acres of pristine desert wilderness in southern Utah, Grand Staircase-Escalante National Monument is a vast and stunning landscape of towering cliffs, deep canyons, and colorful rock formations. Designated as a national monument in 1996, this iconic destination offers visitors a chance to explore some of the most remote and untamed wilderness areas in the American West.

The centerpiece of Grand Staircase-Escalante National Monument is the Grand Staircase, a series of massive rock formations that form a dramatic staircase-like sequence of cliffs and terraces stretching from the bottom of the Grand Canyon to the top of Bryce Canyon. This awe-inspiring geological feature offers a glimpse into the ancient history of the region, with each layer representing millions of years of sedimentary deposition and erosion.

For outdoor enthusiasts, Grand Staircase-Escalante National Monument offers a wealth of recreational opportunities, including hiking, backpacking, and wildlife viewing. The monument's extensive network of trails winds its way through the scenic landscape, offering stunning views of the surrounding rock formations and glimpses of wildlife such as bighorn sheep, mountain lions, and golden eagles.

One of the most popular hikes in the monument is the Lower Calf Creek Falls Trail, which leads visitors through a lush desert oasis to a stunning 126-foot waterfall nestled in a secluded canyon. For those seeking a more challenging adventure, the Escalante River Trail offers a multi-day backpacking trip through some of the most remote and rugged wilderness areas in the monument.

In addition to its natural beauty, Grand Staircase-Escalante National Monument is also home to a rich array of cultural and historical sites, including ancient Ancestral Puebloan ruins, pioneer homesteads, and petroglyph panels. Visitors can learn more about the monument's natural and cultural history through interpretive exhibits, ranger-led programs, and guided tours.

34. Escalante Petrified Forest State Park

Nestled within the rugged landscape of southern Utah, Escalante Petrified Forest State Park is a hidden gem that offers visitors a glimpse into the ancient history of the region. Named for its impressive collection of petrified wood, this unique destination boasts stunning geological formations, scenic hiking trails, and a wealth of outdoor recreational opportunities.

The centerpiece of Escalante Petrified Forest State Park is the petrified forest itself, where visitors can marvel at the colorful remnants of ancient trees that once grew in the area over 150 million years ago. Petrified wood, formed through the process of fossilization, has been transformed into stone over millennia, preserving the intricate details of the original wood grain and texture.

In addition to its petrified wood, the park is also home to a variety of other geological wonders, including towering sandstone cliffs, deep canyons, and unique rock formations. Visitors can explore the park's scenic hiking trails, which wind their way through the desert landscape and offer stunning views of the surrounding scenery.

For those interested in learning more about the area's natural and cultural history, Escalante Petrified Forest State Park features a visitor center with interpretive exhibits, ranger-led programs, and guided tours. Visitors can learn about the process of petrification, the ancient ecosystems that once thrived in the region, and the rich cultural heritage of the area's indigenous peoples.

In addition to its geological and historical attractions, Escalante Petrified Forest State Park offers a variety of recreational activities for visitors to enjoy. From picnicking and wildlife viewing to fishing and boating on Wide Hollow Reservoir, there's something for everyone to enjoy amid the park's stunning natural beauty.

35. Anasazi State Park Museum

Located in the heart of southern Utah's red rock country, Anasazi State Park Museum offers visitors a fascinating glimpse into the lives of the ancient Ancestral Puebloans who once inhabited the region. Situated on the site of a 12th-century Ancestral Puebloan village, this historic site features a museum, interpretive exhibits, and reconstructed archaeological structures that bring the history and culture of the Anasazi people to life.

The centerpiece of Anasazi State Park Museum is the reconstructed ruins of the Coombs Site, a large Ancestral Puebloan village that was inhabited from approximately 1160 to 1235 AD. Visitors can explore the site's excavated rooms, kivas, and storage pits, gaining insight into the daily lives, customs, and traditions of the ancient inhabitants.

In addition to its archaeological attractions, the museum features a variety of exhibits that showcase artifacts, pottery, and tools recovered from the site, as well as interactive displays that provide insights into the Anasazi people's agriculture, architecture, and cultural practices. Visitors can learn about the history of the region, the relationship between the Anasazi and other indigenous peoples, and the impact of European colonization on native communities.

For those interested in further exploration, Anasazi State Park Museum is also surrounded by stunning desert landscapes, with numerous hiking trails, scenic overlooks, and archaeological sites to discover. Whether you're exploring the ruins of ancient villages, hiking through rugged canyons, or simply soaking in the beauty of the desert scenery, there's something for everyone to enjoy amid the park's stunning natural beauty.

Whether you're a history buff, a cultural enthusiast, or simply someone in search of adventure and exploration, Anasazi State Park Museum offers a truly unforgettable experience. With its rich history, fascinating exhibits, and stunning desert landscapes, this iconic destination is sure to leave a lasting impression on all who visit.

36. Capitol Reef National Park

Tucked away in the heart of southern Utah's red rock country, Capitol Reef National Park is a hidden gem that offers visitors a chance to explore some of the most breathtaking landscapes in the American Southwest. Named for its imposing rock formations, which resemble the domes and towers of the United States Capitol, this iconic destination boasts stunning geological features, scenic hiking trails, and a rich array of cultural and historical attractions.

The centerpiece of Capitol Reef National Park is the Waterpocket Fold, a massive geological uplift that stretches for over 100 miles across the desert landscape. This dramatic feature is home to a variety of stunning rock formations, including towering cliffs, narrow slot canyons, and colorful sandstone arches, creating a landscape that is both surreal and mesmerizing.

For outdoor enthusiasts, Capitol Reef National Park offers a wealth of recreational opportunities, including hiking, backpacking, and rock climbing. The park's extensive network of trails winds its way through the scenic landscape, offering stunning views of the surrounding rock formations and glimpses of wildlife such as bighorn sheep, mule deer, and golden eagles.

One of the most popular hikes in the park is the Hickman Bridge Trail, which leads visitors through a lush desert oasis to a stunning natural arch nestled in a secluded canyon. For those seeking a more challenging adventure, the Capitol Gorge Trail offers a rugged trek through towering cliffs and narrow slot canyons, with opportunities for exploration and discovery along the way.

In addition to its natural beauty, Capitol Reef National Park is also home to a rich array of cultural and historical sites, including ancient Ancestral Puebloan ruins, pioneer homesteads, and petroglyph panels. Visitors can learn more about the park's natural and cultural history through interpretive exhibits, ranger-led programs, and guided tours.

Whether you're a seasoned hiker, a history buff, or simply someone in search of adventure and exploration, Capitol Reef National Park offers something for everyone. With its stunning landscapes, diverse recreational opportunities, and rich cultural heritage, this iconic destination is sure to leave a lasting impression on all who visit.

Made in the USA
Middletown, DE
13 July 2025

10592258R00076